Autumn Gold

- Life with Leo -

by

Stephanie Walmsley

Fowey Rare Books
Cornwall PL23 1AR UK.

Fowey Rare Books

4 South Street, Fowey, Cornwall PL23 1AR. UK.

First Published 1995

A U T U M N G O L D - Life with Leo

by

Stephanie Walmsley

ISBN 1 899526 30 7

Typeset and printed by
Alexander Associates
Fowey PL23 1AR. UK.

Autumn Gold - my life with Leo

For Selina with love

Selina Craze

CONTENTS

A boat beneath a sunny sky
Lingering onward dreamily
In an evening of July
Long has paled that sunny sky
Echoes fade and memories die
Autumn frosts have slain July
Ever drifting down the stream
Lingering in the golden gleam
Life, what is it but a dream.

Lewis Carroll

Forward

In writing a forward to Stephanie Walmsley's book I am repaying a debt I owe to her late husband. It is one of which he was unaware, yet which has had a profound influence upon my own life and writing career.

I read Leo Walmsley's delightful book, *Love In The Sun*, when I was living in what was then Rhodesia. Arriving at the last page, I closed the book reluctantly, yet with a degree of excitement. Leo's book, largely biographical, had helped me to make a decision I had been toying with for some time. Suffering whatever fate had in store for me, I would persevere and earn my living as a writer, just as he had.

A year later, I was sweeping floors in a Cornish China clay works in order to live. Yet I never regretted the decision I made then and time has proved it to be the right one.

I have always been grateful for the inspiration given to me in those far off days by this very gifted writer.

Living only a short distance upriver from the creek where Leo had found his isolated home, I was constantly meeting men and women who had known him, known of him, or who had an anecdote or two about Leo Walmsley, *'The writer down to Fowey'*.

I can also claim a brief acquaintanceship with Stephanie and Selina when they were still mourning the husband and father they both adored.

When Stephanie first met Leo, the life he had described in *Love In The Sun*, was behind him. He was by now a highly successful writer. She was a young actress, pursuing a somewhat erratic career with a small and eccentric company.

This is her story.

It is also the story of the happy autumn years of an author who is still regarded with a great deal of respect and affection by those who have read and enjoyed his books. I am happy to be included in this number.

I have enjoyed the insight Stephanie has given into Leo's last years in Fowey. I am confident that the many readers who have derived pleasure from Leo Walmsley's books will enjoy it too.

E.V. Thompson
Cornwall, 1995.

CHAPTER 1.

STEPPING OUT.

The scene is Paddington station. The time is summer-time, July 1952.

My mother and I were hurrying along towards platform three. We hadn't left much time for getting a seat on the train. Everywhere people were hurrying this way and that. The whole place was full of bustle and purpose.

"The train now on platform three is the 11.45 for Penzance, calling at Reading....." The station master's voice was loud and booming.

We followed the porter with the luggage. "I do hope," said my mother who was hurrying to keep with him," that he manages to find you a seat. If only we could have got here earlier!"

Then the porter beckoned us to follow him to a compartment where there was just one empty seat; it was too crowded to take my luggage, that would have to go in the back corridor. Mother thanked the porter and gave him a tip.

"It's a shame that you are not able to have a corner seat," she said, looking round with disgust at the four people who had.

There certainly wasn't much room in the compartment. I was going to be squashed between an enormous woman who was munching crisps and a man with fat legs who was occupying two seats. My mother eyed him reproachfully for a second or two, and then with a bright smile she turned to him and said,

"I wonder if you would mind drawing your legs together so that my daughter can have some room?"

After this I didn't dare look at the fat man, who had moved a fraction, but I was grateful to my mother for putting things right for me and I admired her boldness in dealing with people.

My mother now got off the train which was about to leave at any moment. I went into the corridor and we spoke through the open window.

"Anything you leave behind, I'll sent on."

"Do you think they really will have found digs for me?"

"You've asked me that before and I've told you."

"Yes I know, but just supposing they......"

"Now don't be silly dear. Everything will have been arranged. When you arrive you'll most probably find them all at the station to meet you."

My mother's optimism often baffled me. But this was too much. I stared at her incredulously.

"*All* of them? The entire company?"

"Of course they will."

"Waving flags I suppose and the band playing!" I felt exasperated with her.

My mother looked at me sharply for a second and was about to say something when the whistle blew, taking her by surprise. Then her manner changed, at once becoming mournful.

"Goodbye darling. Don't worry, everything will be all right."

"Goodbye," I said, bending down to give her a hug through the open window. Again the whistle blew.

"You've got enough money," said mother, "to last you for a bit. I'll be anxious to know you've arrived safely."

The train started to move.

"Goodbye," I said smiling at her and blowing a kiss, "Thank you for, well, for everything."

"Don't," she said, beginning to cry and quickly fumbling in her pocket for a hankie. It really stung her when I thanked her like this.

The train was moving faster. I too wanted to cry.

"I'll write," I said, waving hard at her, "Promise." My mother smiled a big watery smile, and waved her hankie until it was almost out of sight. Then I saw her turn and walk away.

Feeling tearful, I went back to the compartment and seated myself next to the fat man and the munching lady. Happily the little bit of room they had made for me was still maintained. I put my hold-all grip on the floor by my feet, unzipped it and took out a thin paper-backed book. I opened the book and glanced round at the rest of my travelling companions. There was nothing very strange or eccentric about any of them. I leant back and closed my eyes for a second.

I didn't know then that my whole life was going to change.

****

Until now I had been working with a repertory company who were performing for a season at a town on the north coast. They had taken over the local theatre and produced a variety of plays. I gained some useful experience. Then the season came to an end and I went home to my parents who were living at a seaside town not far from Folkestone.

Every actor knows that at some time in his precarious career he's going to be out of work, sometimes for months at a time. This is where his agent tells him, "Don't call us, we'll call you." But he tells his friends he is resting.

I suffered no hardship during this out of work period. My parents had a nice house overlooking the sea and life was good. I busied myself by reading Shakespeare, and the plays of Barrie, Shaw and Chekov. I learnt whole speeches from them and practised my dancing. I'd be ready if I got a call for an audition. On fine days I swam in the warm, rough sea, or walked along the cliffs. To keep in touch with the events in the show business world I bought theatrical magazines like "The Stage" and "Spotlight.

Then one day I came in from shopping with a copy of "The Stage" under my arm. My mother was sitting by the open window in our front room. On her lap was a bowl of gooseberries which she was 'topping and tailing'. The sun was sparkling on the sea across the road. You could hear the shrieks of happy bathers splashing each other in the water. The summer was in full swing.

My mother looked up with interest when she saw I'd bought the magazine. She liked it when I read out the ads to her. I sat on the floor and began to scan through the various "wanted' columns. Some had artists themselves advertising their talents. These could be touching or hilarious.

"Oh listen to this one" I said, starting to giggle, "clever, clean lady clown finds herself unexpectedly vacant"'

My mother laughed so much she nearly dropped the bowl of gooseberries.

"We must show this to your father" she said, "go on, read out some more." I read a few more comic ones to her, then I turned over the page. I was silent now for I was looking at an advertisement tucked away among several others that wanted artists for summer shows and reps. This one attracted me. It said simply:

"Artist wanted to Join Fit Up Rep. Touring Cornwall. Sharing Basis." Telephone Fowey...." and they gave a number.

"What does fit up rep mean exactly?" I asked mother, showing her the column. She reached for her glasses which were nearby and took the paper from me. Which one dear? Oh I see it." She studied the advertisement carefully for a few seconds. Then her interest quickened.

"Touring Cornwall.' Oh what fun. I do like the sound of this one."

"We could phone them. They give a number. What an unusual name Fowey. I wonder how you pronounce it."

"Just a minute" said mother, whose interest was growing into excitement now "Why that's the Cornish Riviera! I've heard of Fowey, it's a lovely spot. They have palm trees growing there."

'Have you ever been to Cornwall?"

"No, but your father went to Palmouth as a boy, and loved it." In her enthusiasm my mother forgot my original question so I reminded her.

"You can find all that out by phoning them after six tonight," she said. Soon everything was fixed. On the phone that evening I spoke to a Mr. Howard who said he was actor-manager of the company which he called Howard Productions. They wanted a girl to join them right away. They were putting on the play SEE HOW THEY RUN on Thursday (this was Tuesday). Could come tomorrow? He explained about fit up. It meant they didn't play in one place all the time, but toured around with their props and scenery. There wouldn't be a set salary but the takings each week would be shared out among the company. How strange I thought, that he didn't ask about my qualifications. The part he wanted me to play was Ida the mad maid. Could I think it over, and he would phone back in two hours.

This was something like coincidence. I not only knew the play !and had a copy of it, but I had actually played Ida in the previous rep. company. The play was a riotous romp, a farce with vicars tearing around the stage in their combinations and bishops getting locked in cupboards with prim, church-ridden spinsters. It was all a great giggle and Ida a plump, showy little part, drawing a laugh with every line.

We had a family conference. Mother was in favour of my joining the company. It would be nice for me to be working again and a wonderful chance to see Cornwall. My father was a bit dubious about it, he wondered if I would be properly pald, and who were these people anyway?

But mother didn't want to think of possible draw-backs. She was now so carried away with the idea that she was almost in Cornwall herself.

"If I were young again, how I should love to go", she said, "I've always adored travelling, the thrill of going to new places, making new friends. It wouldn't take me five minutes to pack, and I'd be off!".

"And you know dear", she added, "you've always got your home to come back to if things don't work out".

I think this is what finally decided me, for I made up my mind right then to take the job.

Mother and I spent the rest of the evening sorting out my clothes and packing. We checked up on trains, including those going to London. We'd have a bit of a rush getting from Charing Cross over to Paddington in time for the Cornish train; if we didn't dawdle we should do it alright.

Soon everything was fixed. When Mr. Howard phoned again, I told him I would be joining his company the following day, adding that I already knew the play and had a copy of it. I could almost hear a sigh of relief from the other end of the line. Clearly he had been in a fix trying to find someone to fill the gap. He informed me that the company's head-quarters' would be the Town Hall, where they would be performing all that week.

I asked him to find me accommodation for bed and breakfast, and told him, hopefully, the time of my arrival.

That night I slept so soundly that mother had a job to wake me. She banged loudly on the door several times shouting: "Come on, get up! We'll never do it if you don't. You must get up now if we're to catch the train".

During most of that long journey I studied the play, finding the part of Ida not difficult to re-learn. Now and then I'd look out of the window and be distracted by some quite lovely scenery, or I'd doze off to sleep, waking abruptly when the train came to a sudden halt at a station. Then with guilty feelings I'd resume my studies. But I couldn't entirely prevent my thoughts from wandering. I was excited at the thought of meeting my fellow actors. I was also a bit nervous, and hoped that my acting would be good enough for their repertoire of plays.

My thoughts travelled back to my first professional engagement in show business . . . .

I was two when I made my "debut". Along with my sister, aged four, and a host of other tots, we appeared in a charity matinee at The Mansion House before a distinguished audience including the Queen Mother.

My, sister was dressed as a bumble bee with bright orange wings. She came on and danced a solo. But shortly before her appearance a hushed battle broke out between our mother and aunt as to whether she should wear her long winter woolies under her scanty costume. Mother said yes. The aunt said no.

Finally mother won. The woolleis which h~d been snatched off by aunt were put back. They were rolled up at each thigh in the hope of being hidden. Over them went her costume, a black velvet suit with wings attached at the back.

Halfway through the dance the 'combs' began to make their appearance, first one leg, then the other. Slowly they crept down until they were almost knee level. The audience, delighted, began tittering and nudging each other, and my sister, pink with shame had to carry on dancing with the dreadful sound of laughter coming from the front.

My turn came when I took part in a little number with several other children. We were dressed as toy soldiers and we parade about to the tune of "Dance Of The Tin Soldiers".

Perhaps I was a born comedienne, or maybe it was some perversity which compelled me to do the exact opposite of what I was meant to. And I did it so thoroughly that the audience laughed loudly and thought it was part of the act.

When the other children turned right, I turned left. As they marched forward, I went back. And when they finally marched off (left) I marched off right. T'he Queen must have been amused.

Both my parents were journalists, reporting for the Daily and the Sunday Express.

We lived in a flat at the Prince Of Wales Mansions, Battersea, once inhabited by Noel Coward as a boy.

Mother couldn't look after me and Felicity and keep her job, so we had a nanny. I have hazy recollections of going up and down in the lift to our flat, and being taken to Battersea Park and seeing quite brilliant and wonderful peacocks parading about before us as we sat on a bench swinging our legs.

Because of her work, our mother enjoyed certain privileges. She received complimentary tickets to all the first nights at the theatre and cinema. At Christmas she was given extra tickets for pantomimes, the circus and Peter Pan. We saw them all. Children's fancy dress parties were held at the Mansion House, and the Daily Express organized some too. My sister and I were taken along to these festivities but were a little on the young side to really apreciate them.

We were still quite young when we moved to live in the country. my father had given up reporting. Lord Beaverbrook had begun to take notice of him. Liking the style and clarity of his writing he gave him his chance: to write a weekly humourous column for The Sunday Express. My father took the challenge and in a short time it became immensley popular. It appeared on page three headed in big black type:

SITTING ON THE FENCE
BY
NATHANIEL GUBBINS

I Made my second debut while attending the 'Cone School Of Stage Dancing' in Oxford Street, London. I was thirteen and during the term I lived with my, indulgent aunt Daphne Hughes who had a cosy flat in Mayfair and designed glamorous silk and satin lingerie for rich clients and debutantes. Daaphne was very attractive. She wore clothes that were the height of fashion and had me right under her thumb. She was good to me and I was very fond of her. Sometimes she let me choose a gorgeous nightie or petticoat from stock and altered it to fit me. She took me to the theatre and cinema at weekends, or else we travelled down to Chipstead.

The Cone School was also an agency supplying juvenile artists for plays and films. I was chosen, along with several others to appear in a Christmas play at the Duke Of York theatre. The play, which was set to music, was called 'The Boy Who Lost His Temper'. There wasn't much plot. 'The Boy' sets out on a series of adventures in search of his good humour. On the way he meets dragons, witches, imps and fairies. I was an imp.

Starring in the show was Arthur Askey. The opening scene was a burlesque of a dancing class with Arthur the teacher. He was dressed as typical Dame, with a bonnet and striped bloomers which were well displayed when he held up his skirts, pointed his toe and started to sing:

> "Come now children point your toe
> Use your hands and let them go
> Let your heads sway to and fro
> One two three and away we go."

We danced to his song which had several more verses. Then the boy made his entrance and immediately started to be naughty and live up to the title of the play. He was played by a somewhat precocious lad of thirteen. His aunt, who was in charge of him was constantly standing in the wings ready to prompt him or hand out sweets.

During a break at one of the early rehearsals of the play, the producer took three of the children aside. Then he looked at the rest of us.

"I want one more girl" he said.

We all looked eagerly at him. Theatrical children live in hopes of being singled out for a speaking part or for some speciality turn. I was no exception for I was madly stage struck and used to dream I would one day be a star. Then his glance fell on me.

"You dear" he called. "Little fair girl, come over here".

I was almost trembling with excitement as I went towards him. Then he explained what he wanted. The four of us had been picked out to dance in front of the curtain after the opening first act, while they were changing scenery. We were to be dressed as 'skivvies' waving dustpans and brushes as we danced. Thrilled at being chosen I was determined to do well. The dance was lively and gay. I learnt it so thoroughly at rehearsals that I was able to go over it step by step in my head.

Perhaps I tried too hard for on the first night I danced so violently that I sent my brush flying through the air so that it landed on top of the bald headed conductor in the orchestra.

I don't remember if the show was a great success or not, but the audience seemed to like it and the house was always full. I enjoyed working in the show and I felt quite thrilled when I received my first pay packet.

"Now you're a real professional" my mother told me.

After this 'Cones' got me into a musical called 'Dancing Feet' which was made at Shepperton. It starred a very talented little girl of ten called Hazel Ascot. I was with a bunch of other children from the school. We had a dormitory pillow fight scene which was fun, and when she wasn't performing solo, we danced with Hazel like a supporting chorus. She was a tap dancing wizard. Apart from Astaire, I never saw anyone to equal her speed and precision. We were lost in admiration of her. Some children tried to follow her wherever she went so as to be in her magic circle. The child was never alone. Hurrying on her way to the set she always had a group in attendance. The make-up man, the hairdresser, comb in hand, the continuity girl. Bolder ones among us called out "Hello Hazel!" I loved it all so much. The bright yellow lights, the takes and re-takes, the wonderful 'in talk'—"Right - roll 'em Vince"—"a hundred and forty one take one . . . clap." "I shall always be a part of this world" I told myself, and in my secret fantasy I pretended that I was Hazel Ascot, that glittering little dancing star.

CHAPTER II.

SING FOR YOUR SUPPER.

I must have dozed off to sleep again because the station master's voice woke me by calling out,

"Lostwithiel, change here for Fowey. Train waiting on platform two." This was it, the strange name I had tried to remember. I hurriedly assembled my things together and got out. On the other side of the platform, already waiting, I saw a very small train. It was just one single coach. It reminded me of those in Switzerland that take you up into the mountains. There were only a handful of people in it and it started to go as soon as I got in. The seats were wooden and it was clean and friendly looking.

The little train clattered along, following the Fowey river. It went at an easy pace down a wide estuary, giving time to admire the scenery, which was so enchanting that I felt quite mesmerized as I gazed out of the window. The entire journey had been enjoyable. I had a sense of achievement for I had completely re-learnt the part of Ida in 'See How They Run'. The producer would surely be pleased. I wondered if he would be coming by himself to meet me or whether other members of the Company would be with him. Although I didn't share my mother's optimism in assuming that the entire Company would be on the platform to meet me, I imagined about three or four of them might turn up just out of curiosity.

The train was slowing down now. The journey had only taken about fifteen minutes. I felt a thrill of excitement at the thought of meeting my fellow actors, and I looked out of the window to see if I could spot a group of theatrical people. One can usually distinguish them. But the only people I saw, and there weren't many, certainly didn't look theatrical.

The train stopped. I got out, put my case down and looked up and down the platform. I couldn't see anyone looking for me. It was rather an anti-climax. I began to feel dejected. Perhaps the train was early. In that case I'd better wait around a bit. To make things worse, the other passengers were now being greeted by the people who were waiting for the train. There was much hugging and kissing and 'let me take your bag' and 'lovely to see you' going on. Still I waited, but I couldn't see anyone looking for me. Then the others started going through a small station room to the other side. I decided to follow them. We came out at a drive-in that led off from a tiny main road. Some of the passengers got into waiting cars. I watched them drive off. On the far side of the road, partly concealed by a wall, I saw a large gasworks building. It didn't look very welcoming. Where, I wondered, were those palm trees my mother had spoken of? Parked right near the station were a couple of cars. Their drivers wore peaked caps and looked hopeful. Obviously my best bet was to get a taxi to the Town Hall where surely I would see some members of the Company.

Along a little winding narrow street, with cottages and shops either side, it hardly took us ten minutes to reach the Town Hall. The drive was genial and chatty. Was I a holiday visitor then?. "Sort of" I said. Then I told him what brought me here. Did he know anything about a bunch of actors who had taken over the Town Hall for this week?. No, he couldn't help me there. He'd neither seen nor heard of any theatrical company round these parts. I felt a chill run through me, but firmly suppressed it. The car was slowing down a bit. Looking out of the window on my left, about a hundred yards away, I saw a most attractive quay with boats bobbing about on very blue water.

"Now that over there is The Albert Quay", said the driver, proudly, "named after Prince Albert who landed here in 1846 with Queen Victoria. You'll see it written up on a plaque on the wall directly, when you take a stroll round".

We drove on until we reached the end of street where we turned left, and I saw another quay, wider than the last, but this time we were approaching full on so I saw it more clearly and I noticed there was a rail all round the water side with several people leaning against it.

The driver pulled up against a tall granite building. "Here we are," he said, "Built in the fifteenth century." Then, following my gaze, he added, "Thats the Town Quay. You can hire a boat from there or go on one of they pleasure trips. Now I'll take your case for 'ee."

"Thank you very much," I said, shifting my gaze reluctantly from that enticing blue water, and looking up at the tall building.

"Is this the Town Hall?" I asked.

"That's right m'dear, just you follow me." I followed him to where there was a flight of steps leading up to a solid looking front door. We went up and when we got to the top I noticed the door was open by about half-an-inch. I could here a murmur of voices from inside.

"You'll be alright now," said the driver, grinning at me. I settled up with him and thanked him again for his trouble. He wished me luck and left me to it.

Feeling rather nervous, I took a deep breath and knocked on the door. There was no answer. I tried again, and this time a voice called, "Come in." I picked up my bags, opened the door gingerly and walked in.

The hall was large and there were several rows of hard-back chairs. At the far end from where I stood there was stage and a young man standing on ladder fixing scenery. There was a table near the ladder with a small box on it. At the far right, by the foot of a few steps leading up to the stage, an old woman appeared to be sorting clothes from a laundry basket and handing them to a youngish woman who stood by her side. Both were intent on their job and hadn't appeared to notice me. I walked straight up to the stage, put my luggage down and cleared my throat, hoping to attract the young man's attention.

"Excuse me, but I've come to join the repertory company and I wonder if you know if Mr. Howard, the manager, is here?"

The young man, who appeared to be doing something with a screwdriver, paused for a second to give me and my luggage a brief glance, then with a sort of 'play it cool' smile he said, "You're speaking to him," and resumed his task. He seemed preoccupied and began feeling in his pockets for something, gazing ahead of him as he did so, with remote, steely grey eyes. 'Don't fall over backwards at the pleasure of seeing me,' I wanted to say. But, instead, I said, "Oh" and then "Well, I'm the new girl, I mean....." I broke off, confused. That didn't sound right somehow. I tried again, "I'm Stephanie," I said, "the girl you spoke to on the phone. I've just this minute arrived."

"Hi," said Mr. Howard, without enthusiasm, still keeping his eyes on his job. I looked round rather frantically and saw that the younger of the two women was watching me with a dead-pan expression. She had a cigarette sticking out of the corner of her mouth and her hair was thick and frizzy. I smiled hopefully at her and then turned my attention back to Mr. Howard.

"I've been studying like mad," I told him, "all the way down in the train. I hope I'm pretty well word perfect by now." If he was interested in what I was saying, he didn't show it. However, I carried on. "I'm so glad I got the part of Ida," I said, "because I've played it before in the last rep. I was in. I think 'See How They Run' is a wonderfully funny.....'' I was about to say 'play' when Mr. Howard cut me short.

"We're not doing that play. Plans altered. It's **'Freda'** now. You're Judy. Which reminds me.....'' He turned from his job for a second and shouted, **'MOTHER!'**

Immediately, the elder of the two women answered, "Yes Tony?" She rose from her basket like a well trained dog and came round the front of the stage towards him. She stood at the foot of the stage. Small and frail, she looked up at her great big son.

"You written that part yet?——Judy?"

"Yes Tony. I finished it this morning."

"Let's have it then."

"Very well Tony, I'll fetch it." She turned to go, pausing first to look at me. With a close up view I saw that she was a very old lady. Her face showed traces of a hard life and her eyes looked sad and resigned.

"You must be Miss Gibbons," she said. I let that pass, preferring the name to Gubbins with its comic implications. It was fine for a humourist but tough going for a budding actress.

"I'm glad you've come," said the old lady, without waiting for me to answer. "My son has had so much bother findin' someone to take the last girl's place. She left hunexpectedly when we were playing Stratford On Haven." With those aitches I wondered, What part she was going to play? Then her son called to her to hurry and get cracking. She gave me a rather tragic smile and scuttled off, saying she would be back presently.

Feeling bewildered at the change of plans, I looked to Mr. Howard for further enlightenment. "Mother's gone to get your part," he said, still busy withthe screwdriver, "She's written it out in an exercise book. We haven't got a spare copy of the play, but you'll get the hang of it at rehearsals. There's one tomorrow, here, sharp at ten."

"Is it a big part?"

"So so. It's not the lead."

"When do I have to know it for?"

"We open tomorrow."

"Tomorrow!" I stared at him incredulously. "I've got to learn it by to-morrow!"

"You've got the whole evening."

Was he raving mad? Did he really think I could learn a whole part in one evening?

"You can start right away, soon as mother comes back. **MOTHER!**"
He yelled for her again.

"Coming Tony."

Now came the question that had nagged me for a bit since I started out.
"Could you tell me where I'm staying?" I asked, "Have you got the address?" I wanted to get settled quickly so I could begin work.

"Haven't you got fixed up?"

"No, I haven't. How could I? I mean, I thought you were going to find
some accommodation for me."

"You'll have to look around. I haven't had time to. Been doing this
most of the day."

I could have burst into tears there and then. It really was too much. I
felt quite vexed with my mother and her rosy optimism. Pehaps my father
was right in being cautious. I'd better chuck it and go back home.

I was about to say something indignant when a young man came on to
the stage carrying a roll of posters under his arm. He went over to Mr.
Howard.

"I'm off now," he said, then he saw me and smiled. I smiled back.

"Pass me up that box of nails, Joe, said Mr. Howard. The man took the
box from the table and handed it up to him.

"Right. Now let's have a look." The posters were unrolled. I could
only see from sideways, but the large black type was easy to read. At the
top were the words,

HOWARD PRODUCTIONS
present

"FREDA"

at the Town Hall
on
Thursday, 12th July
at 8 p.m.

The letters which were printed on bright yellow paper got smaller
and smaller as they went down, so I couldn't read the last part.

"Okay. That'll do. Stick them wherever you can, two can go outside the hall, one near the greengrocer's opposite, and one by the Working Men's Institute. Then there's the church railings - fix one there. Then go along the esplanade and stick some along the wall. Just look round generally, and put up as many as you can, some of the shops might let you display them in their windows."

"Okay, Guv." He rolled the posters up again. As he did so, he smiled again at me. He had warm, brown eyes. I felt I could confide in him.

"Hello," he said, setting the posters on the table and sqatting down on his heels, "You just come?"

"Yes," I answered eagerly, "but I've nowhere to stay. Do you know of anywhere?"

"Well, I haven't been here long, but I'm just going out, and if you come along with me perhaps we could find somewhere."

"Oh thanks," I said gratefully, "That would be a help." Luckily just then the old lady came back, carrying a red exercise book, which she held out to her son.

"Thanks, Mother, but I'll have to come down." Then to me, "Can you come up here a minute?"

I climbed onto the stage and he opened the book and showed me the pages of shaky handwriting, which was apparently the part of Judy. Fortunately, it was quite easy to read, but I didn't understand what the half sentences were that preceded my own lines, until I realised they must be my cues. But these were given so briefly, with just the bare minimum of words, that it would take a very clever person indeed to understand what the play could be about. "Just learn them," said Mr. Howard, "and your lines and hope for the best. Joe can tell you what the play's about...."

"But suppose I don't find anywhere to stay? How can I study then? I did think you'd find digs for me." I felt I had a right to be resentful.

The old lady looked anxiously at me and then at her son. But he remained unruffled. "I'm sorry," he said, "but there it is. I just haven't had a minute. You're bound to find somewhere. There are several places that do bed and breakfast. I should start looking now if I were you."

"I'll carry your case," said Joe, "if you take these." So we set off, me with the posters and he with my luggage. As we got to the door, Mr. Howard, who was back on the ladder again, called out. "If you don't find anywhere, you can sleep with mother and me in the van."

14

With these reassuring words in my ears, we stepped out into the evening sunlight. It was just after seven o'clock. Joe fixed a couple of posters outside the hall, one next to the little greengrocer's across the road.

Then we began to search. We walked back through the town, the way I'd come in the taxi, for Joe thought he'd seen some bed and breakfast notices past the post office. He said it was a pity I couldn't stay at his digs, but his landlady was full up. He was up near the other end of the town. He'd only joined the company last week when they were at Stratford. They had all travelled down in the van together. I noticed he had a northern accent.

"I'm from Liverpool," he told me, "One of a family of six." No, he hadn't been to drama school. He'd just wanted to act and had got himself a job before this one, as assistant stage manager in a small repertory company in Wales.

"How many are there in this company?"

"Well, not counting myself, there's Tony, who you met, and his mother, old Mrs. Howard; she works very hard. Then there's Brenda, the one who was sorting the clothes. She's playing the lead." If I was surprised at this, I kept it to myself. "And Jimmy, he's our comic, you'll like him, and a new girl who got here yesterday."

"What's she like?"

"I haven't met her yet."

"Do you know where she is staying?"

"No, I don't. But the others live in the van."

"Good Lord!"

"Yes, it does sound a bit rough I'm afraid, but they have bed-rolls and they're used to it. They all kip down on the floor."

"Is it a large van?" I was fascinated.

"Oh yes, quite large. It takes all their props and scenery. They have a primus stove and cook their food in there as well."

As we approached Albert Quay, I stopped so that I could have another look at that entrancing scene of the blue water and the high land in the distance. I went to the water's edge. Joe came too, and stood looking out.

"I don't think I have ever seen anything quite so beautiful," I said. Joe nodded, "Yes," he agreed, "it is beautiful, and one thing I've made up my mind about. I'm going to have the four seasons here and I'll not go back home until I've seen the Spring come to Cornwall."

Autumn Gold

As we turned to go, I saw a cottage that fascinated me. It was next to the harbour office and there was a dove cote outside the door, which was open to reveal a homely kitchen and a table with a white cloth on it, laid for tea. A plump, pleasant looking woman was sitting at the table cutting slices of bread from a cottage loaf. She must have had her loaf straight from the oven, for right opposite the cottage was a large bakery, adjoining a cake shop.

Lured by the bright cottage and the tempting scene inside, I thought I would ask the lady if I could stay there. "It would be nice to be close to the water," I said to Joe. Joe was doubtful. "But there's no sign outside saying 'Accommodation' or anything."

"I know, but it won't hurt to try. They can only say no." I went up to the cottage.

"Sorry to bother you," I said, "but do you take people in?" I felt like a vagrant. The lady got up and came to the open doorway. She looked puzzled.

"Do I what dear?" I explained my situation. She smiled and shook her head. She was sorry, she couldn't oblige. But she was helpful. "If you go along that road, past the post office, North Street 'tis called, there's a lady at number thirty two who may be able to help 'ee." I thanked her warmly and we set off again.

We had no difficulty in finding the address. It was a cottage on the river side of the street. The lady herself opened the door. She was small with a shiny face and rosy cheeks. She was all smiles and nodding vigorously. "Yes, yes, I could take one easily, bed and breakfast, that's right. Yes I can do that. Would you like to come through?"

It was miraculous. Soon I was being shown into a neat little bedroom with nice old-fashioned rose wallpaper and a large china bowl and jug for hot water standing on a marble topped dressing table. The bed was large and soft looking with a big white eiderdown covering it. But, best of all, the room overlooked the river. I had a perfect view.

After briefing me about the play, and my part, and reminding me about the rehearsal in the morning, Joe left to hang the posters.

Before starting to unpack, I flopped down on the bed and breathed a sigh of relief. I could hardly believe my good fortune in finding such a nice place so easily. I might have fallen asleep there and then if I hadn't been careful. Then I realised for the first time that day that I was terribly hungry. I'd had some cheese and fruit on the train, but I hadn't felt like eating much. It was going to be a long time to breakfast, but I hadn't the time to go out for a meal. I had a little money on me, but as the company worked on a sharing basis, depending on box office takings, I knew I'd have to be careful, not knowing what my share would be. I remembered I had a little fruit left in my grip, so I took out an apple and orange and ate them, looking out at the view.

Presently, there came a knock at the door. It was Miss Sullivan. She wondered if I would like some refreshment after my travels. Perhaps a pot of tea? Would I! I accepted gratefully. It was just what I needed to help me study. She suggested that I came downstairs to where there was a small sitting room also overlooking the water. I went in and sat by the window. In a few minutes she returned bearing a tray with a pot of tea and, to my delighted surprise, a plate of bread and butter. The bread was bright yellow and there were currants and sultanas in it.

"There," said Miss Sullivan, setting the food down on a round table near my chair, "I thought you might like to try some of my saffron cake. Never heard of that I suppose? No, well we use a lot of saffron flour in our baking, help yourself now." I did. It was delicious. A spicy taste with something suggesting cinnamon. I was going to be very happy here.

As I ate, Miss Sullivan chatted to me. She had a fascinating accent reminding me of Devonshire, happy childhood holidays at Babbacombe Bay. I suddenly felt quite blissfully happy. I looked out at the boats going by; dinghies at a leisurely pace, one or two canoes, motor boats chugging along; and the high land across the water. The fairy tale beauty of the place, with whimsical its charm, recalled to my mind the books of my childhood. Waterside stories.....Wind In The Willows.....Beatrix Potter.....and looking at the water I remembered the old magic of Peter Pan's Never-Never land, the eerie enchantment of the mermaids lagoon, beautifully staged, where the illusion of that very blue water was so powerful, that fantasy and reality blended together. Didn't Peter himself, with his brown and green woodland clothes, tunic and tights and curling hat with a feather, resemble a Cornish Pisky?

To the far left across the water, I saw what looked like a small village. I asked Miss Sullivan about it. She opened the window so that I could see better.

"That's Bodinnick," she told me, "only a small place mind, no shops or anything. A car ferry runs continuously backwards and forwards, and goes till quite late in the summer evenings. There, you can just see a glimpse of it leaving the slipway." I saw a quaint attractive looking ferry loaded with cars, and a few pedestrians. To the right of the slipway, by the rocks, was an attractive house with shuttered windows and ivy growing round them. It had a garden and its own slipway and steps down to the water.

"What an adorable loking house," I said, "It looks as though it's been built out of the rock."

"Well, it has," I was told, "They do say, those who've been inside, that the wall at the back of the living room is built entirely from the rock. 'Tis called Ferryside. Miss Angela du Maurier do live there. You'll see her no doubt. rowing across in her boat. She writes, and her sister Daphne du Maurier lives at Menabilly not far from here. I expect you've heard of the du Maurier's?"

"Yes of course I have. I know all about them. There was George their grandfather. He wrote 'Trilby'. And Sir Gerald the actor. I remember my mother telling me she'd been sent to interview him once when she was a reporter. She'd seen him on the stage in Peter Pan."

"Get away!" said Miss Sullivan, "Well, he had that house built for his family. He's dead now but his wife, Lady du Maurier, she lives there too."

I remembered, quite recently, having bought my mother a copy of Daphne du Maurier's novel 'My Cousin Rachael'. She'd simply loved it. My own special favourite of Daphne's books was 'Gerald', a portrait of her father. I thought it showed a real perception and sensitive awareness of his personality and it appealed to me especially as it was all about theatrical people. I had also seen her play 'September Tide' when it came on in London.

Miss Sullivan went on filling me in about the personalities living in and near Fowey. Eric Portman, Mabel Lucy Atwell..... then she pointed across the river to a jutting headland where the river widened into the harbour.

"You can't quite see it from here," she said, "but to the left of that headland going all the way up to Pont, is Pill Creek, and that's where the author Leo Walmsley lives. He has a hut over on the other side of the creek, just above the shore."

Leo Walmsley. The name meant nothing to me then.

"They do say," Miss Sullivan went on, "that he must be terribly lonely at times. He lives there by himself, summer and winter. Every day he comes across in his boat to collect his mail and do his shopping. You're sure to come across him in town. He's written some lovely books. I've read nearly all of them. 'Love In The Sun', that's my favourite. All about Fowey it is, and the little hut across the water."

"Has he always lived alone?"

"Oh,no. He came to live here with his wife, some years back. He tells the whole story of it in that book. The hut was derelict when he found it, and they made all their own furniture. Very quiet it is up there, not a soul in sight. 'Tis beautiful mind, for those who like to be by themselves; no neighbours or anything. Very dark she was , kind of gypsy looking, dark eyes and long black hair. She wore a band round it across her forehead. Some say she had Indian blood in her. They were always dressed alike, same jerseys and trousers. They had a baby, and they used to take it in their boat with them, out to sea. She went around with it strapped on her back, like a papoose."

"How sweet."

"Yes, proper job, that. And just right for the kind of life they led over there, in and out of boats all the time. Very popular she was. A rather high-pitched voice, she had, and popular with everyone. She loved the water and never minded the rain. Then some years later, she left him.....she never came back."

After she'd cleared the table and left me, I didn't think much more about what Miss Sullivan had told me. For one thing, I had this part to learn.

I was about to fetch the book, when the feeling came over me, very strong, that I was meant to come to this place, that somehow it was all familiar to me. This was strange as I'd never been to Cornwall before, and it wasn't that I really believed in destiny or fate; and yet it was a very real feeling, too real to dismiss entirely.

I went up to my bedroom. The bed looked very tempting. The cover had been turned down, all ready for me to get into. I went to the window and opened it wide. I looked far out at the view. There was a sweet smell of honeysuckle in the air and it was beginning to get dusky. Now I understood more clearly the meaning of that feeling I'd had.

"I belong here," I told myself, "Fowey is my place."

CHAPTER III

"KEEP SMILING"

I might have slept on next morning if I hadn't heard a gentle knock on my door. I called out "come in" and groped for the watch by my bed. It was seven o'clock.

Mrs. Sullivan came in with a cup of tea.

"I hope this isn't too early for you but you wanted me to call you when I got up didn't you m'dear? You can have your breakfast at eight or you may like to lie longer and have it at nine."

I could see the bright sun shining behind my curtains.

"I'd like it at eight o'clock please" I said.

Until the early hours of the morning I had been studying my part for the play. I felt I knew most of it, but there were patches where I was a bit shaky.

"FREDA" was an unusual play, and at the time it was written, a controversial one. Set in the period just after the last war, it tells of a typically middle-class family, mother, father, aunt, sons Robert and Alan, and daughter Judy. The eldest son Alan, about to be de-mobbed, is on his way home from Germany where his regiment is stationed. He has met and fallen in love with a German girl, and he is going to bring her home with him. The family reaction to this is the main theme of the play, which, when it first came out had a slogan attached to it: "Would **You** Take Freda Into Your Home?" A thoughtful play with the family feeling of tension and resentment building up as the moment draws near where Alan and the girl are about to arrive. But perhaps it wasn't the ideal entertainment for a summer night at a sea-side resort which offered the rival attractions of boats for hire and pleasure trips.

During breakfast, which was lavish, I did a spot of revision. Although I couldn't grumble at my part, I wished I could have been comic, witty or highly dramatic. I fancied myself pale with ringlets, playing "Camille" or as the mad wife in "Jane Eyre". I didn't quite know what to make of Judy who was just nice, a sweet young thing.

I hurriedly wrote a line to my mother and at a quarter to ten I set off for the Town Hall. The little town was already full of people heading the same way as me. Young couples, families with children carrying prawn nets and such like. All, presumably on their way to the beach. A woman with a small child asked me if I could direct her to Readymoney Cove.

When I got to the hall I thought at first there was no-one there. Then I went round to the right of the stage where I'd seen two women sorting clothes. I discovered a piano behind the curtain and a staircase leading to another entrance. Opposite this I saw a somewhat cluttered room with clothes hanging round the walls and draped across chairs. Obviously a dressing room I thought, and as the door was open I looked in. Old Mrs. Howard was writing at a small table, and the other woman was perched on a laundry basket knitting something, still with a fag in her mouth. In the corner nearest to me by the door, there was a young girl sitting at another table reading from an exercise book. On the table were several sticks of theatrical grease paint, jars of cream and boxes of powder, laid out together with a brush and comb. A good sized mirror was propped up against the wall. The girl had dark brown wavy hair of medium length, casually styled but neat, and dark blue eyes that looked at me with interest when I said:

"Hello."

The old lady turned and gave me a wan smile.

"Tony isn't here yet" she said "but come in and find yourself a corner. This is our dressing room. The men's is next door."

The girl was smiling at me, a big wide humorous smile. I smiled back and we became instant friends. Would I like to share her table? There was plenty of room. She moved her things to one side. I went to get a chair and draw it up to the table.

The girl was called Doreen Sloane and her home was in Cheshire. She had arrived here two days ago. Her father had booked her in at the Fowey Hotel for the first night and now she had moved into digs. She had just finished working with the Liverpool Rep. She had seen the same advert in 'The Stage' and made the same enquiries as I had. It was reassuring to know that everything was as new to her as it was to me. She thought Fowey was a darling little place and hoped we'd have a good audiences.

"I'm your aunt by the way" she said, and giggled.

"You're what! Oh I see." She looked ridiculously young to be anyone's aunt. But she knew the play, having read it some time ago. Did she, I asked, know her lines.

"Oh I do hope so! I've been studying like mad."

At the rehearsal we had the first of many surprises due to come our way while working with Howard Productions. To begin with, it was a little disconcerting to find that our fellow actors were reading from their parts. At least we had banked on *them* knowing their lines! And apart from learning which side to enter or exit we weren't given any stage directions. We had to invent our moves as we went along, and interpret the part without guidance from our producer. Clearly we were on our own.

The rehearsal finished at one o'clock, and we were given the afternoon off until five thirty when we had to be back at the hall for another rehearsal. As we came away I asked my new friend what she thought of the set up.

"Well it wasn't a proper rehearsal was it ?"

"I'd call it a walk through."

"I never expected them to be reading their parts. Whatever's going to happen tonight? And we were a bit shaky ourselves in that scene we have together in the second act."

"We need another full week of rehearsal. Honestly, I've never been in a company like this before."

It was one of those hot, dreamy days you get in mid summer. The little town had a sleepy air, deserted by the holiday makers who had made for the beach and boats. We sauntered along the Town Quay to the water's edge and leant on the rails, watching the pleasure boats filling up. They were having good business that day. I wanted to hire a rowing boat, but we had work to do.

"I'm hungry" said Doreen.

"Let's buy some fruit and cakes and go to White House Beach. Its not far from here, so my landlady tells me. We can study and go over that scene we have together."

We set off looking as though we were on holiday, Doreen in a cool green frock with a big wide belt round her small waist; me in a tyrolean dress I'd bought in Austria. It had the typical low neck, puffed sleeve blouse, and the skirt was raspberry coloured with a pattern of edelweiss flowers. Round this went a pink striped apron. People seeing us might have thought that we hadn't a care in the world. But inwardly I was terrified. How could I possibly, under such conditions give anything near a good performance. I was certain to make a fool of myself. Thank goodness no-one in the audience would know me. I was glad to be anonymous.

It didn't take us more than ten minutes to reach White House Beach which lay sheltered by rocks, near the harbour mouth. From its landing a ferry boat went continuously across the water to the village of Polruan.

As well as fruit we brought cigarettes to help us learn. We settled behind a big rock and tried to block out the happy sounds of bathers splashing and shouting. On such a day it wasn't easy to concentrate. The water so cool, so inviting, made us long to be in it. From where we sat we had a clear view of the harbour mouth where it widened as it met the darker blue sea. There were yachts and cabin cruisers going by and one or two sailing boats which were almost static as there was only the faintest breeze on this perfect summer's day.

Every so often Doreen would cover the page she was learning and shut her eyes and mutter her lines out loud in a maddening way. I had to stick my fingers in my ears.

We kept at it for about two hours and then we went over our scene together at least six times. After a while Doreen slipped off to buy something to eat and returned with bars of chocolate cream. She wanted to climb the rocks. We took off our shoes and stockings. I felt like a kid again with my sister. I'd forgotten what fun it was, up and down the rocks, moving lightly like dancers. We laughed and joked and sometimes stumbled, laughed more and paddled our bare feet in the little pools made by the rocks. The water was nearly warm.

We were young and silly and high spirited. I fancied people were noticing us in our showy dresses. Doreen's laugh kept pealing out whenever we got into comic situations, especially when I slipped and fell plonk into one of the pools. We became quite hysterical when she fell right on to a red faced man sitting on a rock with a handkerchief over his head. The tide was far out and we got quite carried away with our climbing and nearly reached the sandy cove called Readymoney, named after the smugglers who were reputed to have landed there in bygone days.

The intense heat had now gone from the sun, which had moved slightly towards the high cliffs. People with young families were starting to pack up.

"Hey! What's the time?" I said, feeling a pang of fright. Doreen looked at her watch then shrieked;

"Twenty five past! We've got to be there at half past. Quick! Let's run." We had to, it was a mad scramble back through the town. But when we got there we discovered we needn't have rushed. We were just making for the second entrance, nearest the dressing room when we saw a large van parked outside; its back doors were open, and with the exception of Joe, the whole company were seated on the floor eating fish and chips from newspapers.

"You can go up " said Tony, his mouth full "we shan't be long."

Doreen was soon giggling as we got up the steps. "Did you see poor old Mrs. Howard squatting down there by the door pouring all that vinegar over her chips?"

The rehearsal was quickly run through for the benefit of we three new-comers. The other members of the company were apparently not in need of it as the play was in their repertoire. We were more sure of our scene in act two and Doreen had a lot of confidence as well as being a good actress. Joe gave sincerity to his part as Robert the younger son but the others were still reading from their scripts. I wondered if they would still be holding them when the curtain went up.

It was now six thirty and I had to rush back to my digs for my make up and clothes. As the play was not a period one we could wear what we liked. I selected a few pretty frocks for 'Judy' and got back to find 'Aunt Nell' peering at herself in the dressing table mirror, and sprinkling white talcum powder over her hair which had been drawn back into a bun. It now looked suitably grey.

"That's marvellous" I exclaimed, looking at her reflection.

"You look quite different."

She laughed, made a comic face and put a few more touches to the lines she had drawn from nose to mouth. Then a few crow's feet were etched in under her eyes, and tram lines across her forehead. Because her clothes were on the young side, Mrs. Howard had found her a nice middle-aged tweed skirt and one of those vee necked cardigans that slope drearily down to the waist and fasten in front by about four buttons.

My turn to get ready now. I had little to do except to put on a simple frock with a demure white collar and matching Alice band for my hair which I brushed until it shone. Next, the make-up and I was ready.

The leading lady had changed into a navy linen suit with a matching coat and a rather smart hat perched over her abundant hair. As she didn't make her entrance until quite late in the play, she had the job of selling programmes, while old Mrs. Howard, who was wearing a curiously long black dress and head scarf, had to take tickets at the door. They went off together. It was nearly seven o'clock.

Doreen was surveying her new image in the looking glass. Holding a hand mirror she turned first one way, and then another. "Do you" she said, turning right round to see her back view "like Brenda?" I was a bit bothered because the heel of my right shoe was loose. I didn't want to fall smack on my face when I walked on to that stage.

"I don't really know her yet. She does stare so doesn't she, all the time I was getting changed she was staring."

"I think Jimmy's nice. He usually plays comic parts and I've heard that he's very funny." Jimmy was playing the father in the play to Mrs. Howard's 'mother' while Tony had the male lead as Alan the elder son.

"Did you notice how big their van was inside? I suppose it would have to be. But fancy that poor old lady having to sleep on the floor."

"And she's seventy five, Joe told me."

Quaint old-fashioned music was coming from a musty gramophone. Then the slightly cracked voice of a man singing "Underneath The Arches."

"They ought to be coming in soon" said Doreen, "shall we go and have a look?"

We went up and peeped through the curtain. About fifteen people were already seated on the hard backed chairs. I noticed a nice looking family, several young people, boys and girls, sitting at the back, some older people towards the front and a very smart looking woman smoking a cigarette from a holder. She gazed round the hall with a bored expression. An attractive man was sitting next to her. The blinds were drawn over the windows, shutting out the evening sunlight. I began to feel very unsure of myself, my part and my shoe. Brenda was trying to sell a programme to the smart woman who didn't look a bit interested. But the man beside her fished in his pocket for some change and bought one.

"Come on" I whispered to Doreen "I've seen enough. Let's go back." The stage was set quite attractively for the first act. There was a small settee down centre and a sideboard to the right of it; to the left an easy chair. At the back, upstage, a clever bit of scenery suggested french windows with a door on either side.

A different tune was coming from the gramophone now. The cracked voice man was singing "Little White Lies."

We went back to the dressing room and had a quick run through of our scene. Then Mrs. Howard came back with Brenda.

"Fillin' up nicely now" she said, "About a hundred out there. It's half past seven, and we'll be starting in a minute, soon as they stop coming in."

To me she added "I hope you're ready dear?" We were both on early in the first act where the curtains draw back to discover 'father' seated on the settee doing a cross-word puzzle from a folded newspaper on his lap. Then on comes 'mother' with a vase of flowers which she places on top of the side-board. I had little to do in this scene except to breeze in, utter a few lines and breeze out again. All the same I was dreadfully scared. I put a few touches to my make up.

"I wish I could fall in a faint" I said.

The gramophone stopped playing, everything went deathly quiet. Then a knock on our door. "You're on mother" said Tony. The old lady went up the steps to the foot of the stage. I followed with Doreen who wasn't on yet but wanted to watch. The lights went out in the front. Joe was standing in the wings ready to draw the curtains back. The footlights came on. Tony from across the stage waited to signal to Joe. 'Father' had taken his position. Then up with Tony's hand and back with the curtains. Someone in the audience coughed. Mrs. Howard went on with the vase of flowers.

The play had begun.

"Oh heavens, my mind's gone blank!"

"Sshh....you're nearly on."

It's always a ghastly moment when you go on and say that first line in a new play, whether it's Drury Lane or a town hall. The hall is really worse, for you are more aware of the faces watching, can see them more clearly. But to learn a part at the last minute, from a play you haven't read, would tax the power of the greatest actor.

I watched Mrs. Howard put the flowers down and arrange one or two. I was like a sprinter before a race. Up came my cue.

Doreen gave me a friendly push. "You're on now."

I remember mother's advice dinned into me through the years "always smile— it's a passport through life" so I went on with this big toothpaste effort hoping the audience would like me.

Somehow I got through without any dry ups, and when I came off Doreen was smiling at me.

"Thank God that's over, was I awful?"

"No, you were fine, really, you did very well." I could hardly believe her but I felt encouraged. Her turn next. I hung around waiting. Mrs. Howard was having a big scene with 'father' about their eldest son. She was dropping her aitches all over the place.

Keep Smiling

Doreen's cue was coming up now. Having told me how nervous she was I was surprised to watch her go on and say her lines with a definite technique and assurance. She stood out as a professional.

"And you knew your lines better than the others" I told her afterwards.

"Don't talk too soon, we're not through it yet."

So far the play wasn't going too badly. The audience, stoical on their hard chairs, sat politely through the first few scenes, while the evening sunlight flickered on the drawn blinds.

We had reached the interval now. Tony put on another scratched record. Two youths at the back saw their chance and beat it.

Back in the dressing room we got ready for our scene together. We lit cigarettes. I changed my frock. There was just time for a last look at the lines. Then the music stopped.

"Hurry you girls." Mrs. Howard looked fussed.

We stubbed our Woodbines and went up. I settled on the small sofa, 'Aunt Nell' in the easy chair. The curtains went back.

Now everything was going nicely until we got to the bit where Aunt Nell should say, "it's all been a great shock for your mother" and Judy replies, "Yes, she'll never forgive Alan for this." Mother has received some poison pen letters about the German girl and Aunt Nell is showing them to Judy. Then she folds them up and puts them in her handbag. I looked at Aunt Nell and waited for my cue......and waited. My look was returned with a blank stare. Oh God, she's dried up I thought. Luckily my line was one that could be said at random. The silence was electric, unbearable. I decided to go ahead.

"Mother will never forgive Alan for this" I said, shakily. There was no answer. She was completely stuck, even after getting her cue. I felt we were both drowning. Then I saw her shoulders shake: she was making curious whimpering noises. Was she crying?

I soon discovered she wasn't crying. *She was laughing.*

I didn't dare look at her anymore. A man in the audience lit a cigarette. Someone muttered something. I sternly told myself to think of something sad immediately. A snort came from my aunt. I bit hard on my lip. 'Funerals' I told myself, 'earthquakes',' children starving.'

The suspense was mounting. I heard someone from the audience give a decidedly irritable sigh. Stealing a glance I saw that it was the smartly dressed woman with the bored eyes.

Autumn Gold

I was wishing someone would prompt Doreen when it came in the form of a strange hissing noise from the wings. But she was in no state to pick it up. The hissing continued, louder, and dreadfully audible to the audience.

There was nothing for it but to plunge straight in to my next line which was curiously apt:

"I feel" I said, in a queer voice that seemed to come from the top of my head, "as though the whole world is looking at me through binoculars."

I don't recall the line that should have preceded that strange remark, only that it caused havoc. Doreen, convulsed, suddenly rose from her chair and bolted, leaving me exposed, vulnerable on the sinking ship. She was immediately pushed back on again by old Mrs. Howard, a cruel punishment which only threw her further off balance.

"That was the telephone " she said, in a voice that could have fooled no-one. She went back to her chair.

"Really!" my surprise was genuine, "who was it?" This was a mean one but it slipped out.

"Oh...er...as a matter of fact it was Alan... to say he'd been delayed." She was floundering wildly "They'll be an hour late." A dreadful blunder. Alan was due on the stage any moment. I said "Oh" for there was nothing else I could say.

Angry mutterings could be heard off stage. Another hideous pause. Then Doreen remembered the vital line which put us back on the right course.

We carried on until we got to a point where old Mrs. Howard makes noises off, my cue to say "I think I heard something." I listened for the noises, but all was deadly quiet. What could have happened? I'd better jog her memory I told myself, and I took my line.

"I think I heard something" I said, with a frantic look at the wings. But the only sound you could have heard was a pin drop. The silence prevailed. I decided not to wait but to carry on. I got up, went over to the french windows and looked out. Now this was Alan's cue to come straight on through the door at the right hand side of the windows. I went to this door and flung it wide open in readiness.

"Alan" I cried, "you've come!" With arms outstretched I went forward to greet him. But the doorway was empty. I stood there paralysed.

Noises off were heard.

Then: "Hello everyone!" I turned round, bewildered, to see Alan walking on behind me from the wrong side.

****

Keep Smiling

We were in a cafe eating egg and chips. Doreen was making a sand-wich of her chips between bread and butter. The horrors of the evening were being re-lived:

"Wasn't it awful!"

"I could have died!"

"Your face when you discovered......."

We had been longing to get out of the dressing room out of earshot of the old lady and Brenda, so that we could talk it over.

Doreen was apologetic about leaving me stranded on the stage. So far Tony hadn't said anything to her about it. He might be quite furious she thought.

"I shouldn't think so " I told her "seeing that he forgot his cue and made a hash of his entrance."

"Did you notice a girl in a white sweater in the front row? She was crossing and uncrossing her legs and getting more and more impatient and disgusted every minute."

"You know that couple who came round and introduced themselves after the show? I think they said they had an antique shop across the wa-ter."

"Yes, well did you notice they never mentioned the play?"

"Or our brilliant performances!"

"It's hardly surprising."

"Am I glad its over, for tonight anyway."

We worked out our resources and discovered that we could just afford to finish off with coffee and cakes.

More chat about the play, then when we got up to go I remembered I'd left some things in the hall which I needed.

We walked back together. When we got to the entrance we saw Joe just coming out. He would wait for us he said.

As I collected my things from the dressing room I breathed a sigh of relief. "Just think we won't have to sit up half the night studying."

On our way out we saw Tony leaving the men's dressing room. "I meant to give you these before you left " he said. He handed us each an exercise book. "Your parts for tomorrow night. We're doing **Wuthering Heights**."

****

CHAPTER IV.

LEO'S ENTRANCE.

If it had been a shock to be told at the last minute that I was going to appear in a straight comedy instead of a crazy farce, the news we had just received was even worse.

We walked slowly to the Town Quay, Doreen, Joe and I. We were stunned. How on earth, we asked each other, does one learn a whole new part overnight? We wondered whether to confront Tony and suggest he was making unreasonable demands. We talked it over sitting on one of the seats overlooking the harbour. After a while we decided to go back to our various digs and look at the parts we had been given. If they were not too big then we would do our best.

The following morning Doreen and Joe arrived red-eyed at rehearsal, but they had decided to go through with it. In the play Doreen was cast as **Isabella**, not such a large part as the leading role of **Cathy** but enough to have kept her up half the night with black coffee and cigarettes.

Joe was to double the parts of **Edgar Linton** and **Heathcliff's** son **Hareton**.

I was the more fortunate, having been given the part of Cathy's daughter, a girl of about fifteen, and I had only to appear in the last act with Joe. It hadn't taken me long to learn my lines and it would be a nice easy part to play.

Once again Brenda had the lead, with Tony as Heathcliff. The remaining characters were to be played by Jimmy and Mrs. Howard, with any alterations made that Tony saw fit. For example, old Mr. Earnshaw underwent a 'change of sex' in order to be played by Mrs. Howard as there wasn't another man available.

We rehearsed all morning. I realised then that those who were reading from their scripts were doing so out of habit, as it became obvious that they were familiar with the play. At one point Doreen was almost in tears saying that she did not think she could carry on. But I was full of admiration for the amount of studying she had done and how much she knew.

At one o'clock we knocked off, with a short break for lunch. There would be a further rehearsal in the afternoon. We walked towards a cafe,

Leo's Entrance

the three of us. Doreen was dispirited. She felt she was being asked to do the impossible. Joe said that the real brunt of learning these plays at short notice was falling on us three. The others in the company had worked together for years and it was part of their repertoire.

We aired our grievances over hot cornish pasties and coffee until it was time to return to the hall. In the dressing room we found Mrs. Howard sorting out period costumes for us to try on, low necked velvet dresses with a tight bodice and lots of tiny buttons down the front. The skirts were full to the ground. Doreen was given a shawl to fasten in front with a broach. She cheered up when she saw herself in this outfit for the dresses had a quaint charm; they put us in the spirit of the play.

The rehearsal, a quick run through, went well the second time, and at four o'clock Tony told us we were free until seven.

During one of my brief appearances I had a song to sing, a verse of an old English air called Bobby Shaftoe which I knew.

Doreen was in the dressing room making an alteration to one of her costumes. I had learnt my part, and I was sitting at the piano trying to pick out this tune. Then I began playing some classical pieces learnt from childhood.

On this particular afternoon while I was having fun with Chopin and getting quite carried away because I loved music, I only half heard a voice say:

"I hope I'm not disturbing you. You must be one of the actors? What a nice touch you've got." The voice was deep and assured. I looked down and saw a man coming halfway up the stairs. He was smiling at me, a gentle half amused smile. He had a lot of thick brownish grey hair with a wave on top, and an old rucksack was slung across his shoulders. I guessed his age as forty eight. "Don't stop" he said "it sounds lovely."

But I did stop, and smiled at the stranger wondering who he was.

"Look, I'd better introduce myself". He slipped the rucksack off his shoulder and put it down. Just then Tony and Joe came off the stage. They were about to go down the stairs but on seeing the man they paused at the top and looked down at him with interest.

"Sorry if I seem to have barged in on you" he said "but I've been trying to work up my courage to call on you people. My name's Leo Walmsley. I write books." He looked round shyly at us, then added:

"Don't be embarrassed. You haven't heard of me! Well I'm rather a

31

forgotten man at present. Trying to make a come-back. I'm in the middle of a new book."

He went on to say that he had a daughter who had been to the Royal Academy Of Dramatic Art and was now in repertory encountering some rather poor houses. It was thinking of her that made him call to see if we were getting good support. Tony started telling him about the company, about **Freda** and the play we were putting on tonight. You could sense his genuine interest as he listened.

Lured from the dressing room by the sound of voices, Doreen came to join us. She looked at the visitor with surprise, and then, with suppressed giggles, at me.

"Ah" he said "another one! How many of you are there?" He looked benignly at her and I introduced them. As they spoke I took a closer look at the man. He had a large full mouth and thick dark eyebrows. His eyes were deep set, hazel coloured with a light in them. The expression was gentle. He was wearing a rather worn out jacket over corduroy trousers, a patterned red scarf and big wellington boots. I must have been staring rather hard at him for he was looking at me when he said:

"I have to dress rough for the kind of life I lead. I live across the water and I spend a lot of time in my boat, my one form of transport. I'm hoping to catch a fish for my cat on the way home."

It dawned on me then that he must be the author who lived in the hut on the shores of Pill Creek, the one my landlady had told me about, who rowed across to Fowey for his shopping.

He said, "Look, I must be off now or my boat will be aground. I'm glad I came along. It's been grand meeting you. I can't come and see you tonight but I'll come on Saturday when the tide will be right." He bent to pick up his rucksack, "You've got me excited now," he said, hoisting the strap over his shoulder, "I just love the theatre. I'm thinking now of my own play **Sally Lunn**. Never heard of it I suppose? It's a good play." He looked away reflectively. "It was put on at the Grand Theatre, Halifax, some years ago, and produced by the West Riding Arts Council. They did it very well."

To me he said: "You would make a marvellous **Sally**."

He spoke of his new book, and the one with Fowey as its setting.

"That was my best seller. How ironic. And here I am, almost a forgotten man".

Again he looked at me and smiled: "I must write and tell my daughter about this" he said, and then he was away down the steps and hurrying off to the boat.

To my shame I hadn't read any of Leo Walmsley's books.

"Wasn't it kind of him to call", said Doreen. "At first I thought I was going to burst out laughing. He looked so strange in those funny clothes. Did you notice how wild his hair was, like a chrysanthemum."

"That old rucksack slung across his back! But what a striking voice, like a Shakespearean actor."

Tony didn't say anything and went off to see about the props, first reminding Joe to distribute the new posters advertising **WUTHERING HEIGHTS**. Doreen went back to her digs to study and I went with Joe to help.

After that I did not think much more about the man with the actor's voice and rugged face. Joe and I were kept busy pinning the posters.

Shortly after I got back to my digs Doreen dashed in, frantic for me to hear her lines.

Surprisingly the play went well that night. There were more people in the audience and the sun had gone behind the clouds early which promised well for the box office.

Tony swaggered and strutted round the stage in magnificent arrogance as **Heathcliff**. Doreen coped wonderfully with **Isabella**. There were no serious dry-ups, but she breathed a sigh of relief when it was over.

Outside the night air was soft and cool. I waited for Doreen who was taking her make-up off. I had to deliver a bombshell to her and I wasn't looking forward to it.

I went over to the waterside and leant over the railings. There were yachts, cabin cruisers and dinghies, all different sizes. The water was calm. I wanted more than anything then, to haul in one of those dinghies and pull round the harbour.

During supper at our usual cafe, Doreen chatted away. She was triumphant at having learnt her part.

"That scene I had with Tony. I'd been dreading it. But I think I only dried up twice."

"I know. You were marvellous."

"I don't think many people could have done it: take you for instance. I don't say you couldn't have acted the part alright, but could you have learnt it at all? Kept yourself awake half the night? I doubt it. I think I'm that bit quicker than you, don't mind my saying so. Anyway," she stirred her coffee triumphantly, "I've proved I can do it."

I decided to bring her down.

"Looks like you're going to have to do it again" I said smugly. "I didn't like to tell you before, but just as I was leaving the hall, Tony gave me this." I handed her the book. "It's for you, he told me to tell you that we're doing **Love On The Dole** tomorrow and you've got the leading part!"

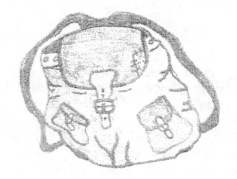

CHAPTER V.

DOREEN'S DILEMMA.

The mournful cry of seagulls woke me next morning. I turned over and groped for my watch on the bedside chair. It was just after seven with the sun already shining. Time was precious, the morning too beautiful to waste in bed. I got up and dressed quickly; Joe had told me that we might not be staying long in Fowey. This was a good chance to have a walk through the sleepy little town while it was semi-deserted.

All the seaside resorts rely on fine weather for a good season. Fowey was no exception with her hotels, boarding houses and pleasure boats.

From the actor's point of view there was nothing better than a nice rainy evening for 'pulling them in'.

But I could sense an oncoming heatwave as I walked along the narrow street. On my right I passed an old Wesleyan chapel built in 1894, then I came to the turning where the road veered sharply to the left. I passed the post office, a Queen Ann house and the customs office. I wanted to get a glimpse of Pont Creek so I made for the Albert Quay. The tide was high with the water nearly up to the top steps. Looking across I saw that Pont Creek was obliterated by the jutting headland dividing it from Fowey river. Better to try the other Quay. On my way I passed a sixteenth century Tudor style house. It had lattice windows and a heavy oak door.

At the Town Quay I had a good view of the opposite side. From the shore there was high land rising more than twenty feet and covered in bracken, with oak trees at the edge of the cliffs.

At the top of the land there were sloping fields. Part of Pont Creek was visible; wide at the entrance it narrowed past the headland, and there, nestling between some trees, I saw a pink roofed cottage. There was a slipway leading up to it from the water where a dinghy was moored. It all seemed to add up to the description my landlady gave me of Leo Walmsley's home.

A rugged face, a ruck-sack and gum boots. My impression of the fisherman author. I suddenly remembered he was coming to watch the play tonight. He was going to get a surprise, thinking we were doing 'Wuthering Heights'. And he wouldn't see much of me. Cast as a newspaper boy all I had to do was make a few entrances, shouting in a loud voice: "**READ ALL ABOUT IT, READ ALL ABOUT IT.**" One has to be willing to do anything in repertory, but I couldn't help thinking that on this occasion, it was bad luck I should have only a walk on part. And there at the other extreme was Doreen, landed with a whacking great part that she couldn't do justice to. Normally, any actress would be thrilled to get the lead in a fine play like **Love On The Dole.**

The title of the play made me think about finance. I wondered if I had enough money to last until we got paid.

I stood for a while looking across at the enchanting view. Then I turned away from the Quay and continued my tour. I passed the entrance to the historic old parish church, set back from the street, turned a corner to the right by a pub, and went up Lostwithiel Street, passing shops and cafes until I came to the Esplanade which was on the level. This was the ultra respectable end of town, soon to be full of people and cars making for the sea. On my right were the large hotels and boarding houses, as well as residential ones, and to the left, after the drive down to White House Beach, there was a clear view of the harbour and Polruan.

I kept along the left side for about a mile, following the harbour until I reached a sandy cove situated at the harbour mouth, with rocks at either side. Set back from the cove were a few cottages and behind them some woods. I looked round, absorbing the loveliness of the place. The cove was just as deserted as the town. The walk had made me hot. I sat down on the sand. How cool the water looked.... I kicked off my shoes. Then without a second thought I pulled off my skirt and blouse and plunged in. In a second I bobbed up again, shocked, gasping with cold. The enticing blue water was deceptive. I swam a few strokes then, shivering, I stumbled back to shore. The early morning sun wasn't hot enough to dry me so I flicked the water off with my skirt and ran about for a bit. Soon I was warm again and feeling good. Now I wanted to explore further, to venture into the woods and follow on where the notice read **TO THE CLIFFS**. I had heard there was a lovelier place than Readymoney Cove. It was called Pridmouth and you reached it by walking along the coastline.

But I knew there was an early morning rehearsal call for **Love on the Dole** and I did not want to be late. I dressed quickly and walked back. By the time I reached my digs I was glowing.

At the rehearsal I found Doreen scared and unhappy. She had stayed up nearly all night with a thermos of black coffee.

"I've only been able to learn the first act", she told me. For the rest of the play she was all at sea and reading her lines from the exercise book of cues.

Doreen's Dilemma

Tony, preoccupied with his own part, seemed unaware that his heroine did not know hers.

As usual we had a couple of hours off in the afternoon. It was now scorching hot. Doreen went to my digs, to try desperately to learn the rest of her part. I went with Joe to hang the posters.

When I got back it was panic. Doreen was frantic. She had the book on her knees and a whole pile of cigarette stubs beside her. She looked up at me with a pathetic expression:

"I can't learn it. I keep on going over and over it, but it's such a big part. Whatever am I going to do?"

Sally Hardcastle was not only a big part to learn, but also demanding. In a sense she dominated the play, being on stage in nearly every scene.

"Let me hear you" I said, taking the book from her. "How far have you got?"

"Up to here." She pointed to the page. It was the second act. I began feeding her the cues. She started off alright and I was about to congratulate her, when she dried up. After that she kept floundering. It got worse and worse. Finally she burst into tears:

"It's no good, I can't possibly learn it all. I haven't had time." I handed her a cigarette, taking one myself.

"Shall I have a word with Tony? I'll say you're not well." She grew quieter, puffing hard on her cigarette. Then she said:

"Perhaps you could tell him I've sprained my ankle?"

"Would he believe you?"

A mad idea came to her."Suppose I really sprain it. I could jump out of the window!"

I looked at her in horror, "Are you crackers?"

"I don't mean from here, but the room where you have your breakfast isn't far from ground level. The window can't be more than six feet from the grass below, so I couldn't hurt myself badly, just enough to stop me going on tonight."

She really must have been desperate. I thought of the comic side and nearly laughed:

"Whatever would my landlady think if she was in the garden and saw you leaping out?" Doreen had to smile.

"She might think it was hallucinations." We finally agreed that I should present him with the true facts.

I hurried along to the town hall. He was on the stage fixing scenery.

"Doreen is terribly upset," I began, "She's asked me to tell you she can't learn her part for tonight, she's tried awfully hard and doesn't want to let you down. But she hasn't had enough time. She's crying and says she can't go on."

Tony was unmoved. "She'll have to" he said, curtly, "Tell her to do her best."

This was terrible. I tried reasoning with him, pleading, but it was useless. He was adamant. I walked back wondering just how I could face Doreen with the news. When I finally managed to tell her she became more frantic than ever.

"Oh its not fair!" she cried, "I've only learnt half of it. I can't go out there and make a fool of myself."

She began to think of some more suicide suggestions and then I said, "Look this is how I see it. No one can force you to go on. Either flatly refuse to, or else go all out and make a desperate effort to cram in the rest of your lines."

She thought for a moment. Then she said, "Alright, I'll take a chance on it. What's the time?"

I admired her pluck. It was now four o'clock.

"Oh heavens! Will I ever learn it?"

"I've heard a wet towel helps!" I quickly got mine and dabbed it in the water jug. She wound it round her head.

"Start now. I won't interrupt you for we'll both be busy. I've got to do something to stop my trousers falling down."

For my brief part as a newspaper boy, Mrs. Howard had fished out some men's clothes. They were much too big, but I could roll up the sleeves of the sweater and the Gatsby cap was quite becoming. I held the trousers against me, wondering how best to take them in.

"It's alright for some" said Doreen, surveying both me and the pants with a gloomy expression.

"It's not you know. I've only got one mouldy line to say in the whole play. I shall feel such a fool..... still, never mind, we'll be laughing about it all afterwards. Think how we laughed at the end of **Freda**."

"We were hysterical."

"After all, it isn't as though the play will be performed on a big London stage like Drury Lane or the Haymarket Theatre. Or even in a big provincial town like Leeds or Manchester. We're just playing in a town hall."

"Not even a big one."

Doreen's Dilemma

"Although there's something about Fowey that sets it above other holiday resorts. It's a town of quality."

"But just think " said Doreen brightening, "how much worse we would feel if we knew that, say, Eric Portman was in the audience tonight, or Daphne du Maurier. As it is neither of them is likely to turn up, or for that matter, any other distinguished per......." She broke off abruptly, clapping her hand in front of her mouth. We stared at each other.

"Oh **No!**" Doreen let out a shriek of horror. "I've just remembered. Leo Walmsley! **He's coming to watch the play tonight!**"

At the main entrance to the Town Hall (there were two of them leading to this fifteenth century building) old Mrs. Howard was selling tickets at a small table just inside the door.

Inside the lights were on, the stage all set. "When you and I were seventeen......." sang the cracked voice man on the gramophone. In the dressing room Doreen was muttering her lines over and over like someone demented, her eyes glassy with fright. She had learnt the gist of her part but she wasn't taking chances. All the way up the inside of each forearm she had written, in ink, lines that she hadn't been able to learn. This had escaped the notice of our producer; it was hoped it would be the same with the audience.

Tony had told me to go out front selling programmes. I wore a cool summer frock as I did not have to change into the boy outfit until later on. We were running late. So far I had only shown half-a dozen people to their seats. Perhaps the title of the play was putting people off. To attract happy holiday makers on a Saturday night over bank holiday week-end it might have been wiser to present a jolly farce.

I looked at my watch. It was coming up to eight o'clock. The play was due to start. I went backstage to see what was happening. I found Tony peering through the curtains, counting the house. If he was anxious he didn't show it for his expression was blank, inscrutable. "If we don't get any more in we may have to chuck it" he said, as though to himself. Joe put another record on. I went back.

As I was going out of the door to the right of the stage I saw a man standing at the back of the hall waiting to be shown to his seat. From the distance I did not recognise him, then as I went up the aisle to take his ticket, I saw the weather-beaten face, the deep set eyes with their soft look, and I smiled.

"So the tide was right after all."

He greeted me warmly and I sold him a programme. He was very smartly dressed wearing a rust coloured pullover and yellow tie, his hair with a becoming wave on top. I showed him to his seat. My heart felt a pang as I surveyed the audience of six. If only more people would come. I went and stood hopefully by the entrance, waiting.....and waiting. It was now after eight; now unlikely that any more people would turn up. I felt I could safely risk telling Doreen that Leo Walmsley was in the audience.

Again I went backstage. This time I found the company huddled together having a conference. Tony was addressing them in a low voice. On seeing me he said, "The play's cancelled." Then he went on stage and regretfully announced his decision, apologising to the audience and asking them, would they please call at the box office where they would have their money refunded.

Afterwards he told the company that there would be a meeting tomorrow morning, apart from that we had a free day.

Doreen looked like a prisoner who had just received a last minute reprieve. After a while we both felt a sense of anti-climax; the worry, the mounting tension; we had been so keyed up that it had prepared us, at least Doreen, for action.

We hung around for a little bit like deflated balloons. There was no prospect of supper at our usual cafe. We were broke. Joe thought we might get paid when the takings of Thursday and Friday were shared out in the morning. There was nothing for it but to have an early night.

In my own interest I could hardly be sorry about the play. But I had hoped I might have a word with Mr. Walmsley who had been so kind to come and give us his support.

I did not have to change or take make-up off so I was the first to leave the hall. Just as I was coming out of the other entrance I saw him again. He appeared to be waiting for someone and when he saw me I thought I saw his face light up. He would like to talk to me, he said. I smiled at him.

"I hope you're not too disappointed about tonight's flop."

"I am rather; but you can blame the fine weather for keeping people away."

"You must get your money back.....for your seat."

He looked embarrassed:

"I have as a matter of fact, but I felt rather awful about it."

We chatted for a bit about the stage. Briefly I told him about my acting career in repertory, musicals and pantomime. Then I told him about my father. At first he could hardly believe it.

"Don't tell me you were **THE AWFUL CHILD**?"

"Yes. Meet the monster in person."

"Good Lord! This is exciting. **THE AWFUL CHILD!**" Why, in that case he knew me already. How he had laughed at her and all the other characters in **The Sunday Express**. He only bought the paper to read Nat Gubbins.

I went on to tell him about the present company and the dramatic events of the afternoon. He confessed to being surprised at seeing the poster advertising tonight's performance, not thinking our repertoire could change so quickly.

"I doubt if I could learn a part in four weeks, let alone one a night," he said.

With diffidence he asked if I would like to celebrate the occasion with a drink, adding that I must not misinterpret his motives for he was quite respectable; true, he was married, but his wife had packed up on him eight years ago taking the children with her.

I felt honoured at the invitation. "I should love to," I said.

We set off, round a corner, near the church gates and up an avenue with trees on either side. The pub we were going to was at the top of the hill. Walking along, Mr. Walmsley told me something of his unhappy domestic affairs. He never ceased to hope that his wife would one day return, for the life they had shared in Cornwall held special memories for them. Now all his hopes were centred on his little son Shawn, the youngest of his children, who was supposed to be coming to stay with him. His wife was insisting he had a house-keeper for the holiday and he was anxiously waiting to hear from a friend who had helped out before.

The hill was steep but he walked up easily with a light step. However, when we reached the top he hesitated.

"I never feel quite right going into a pub. My mother was very religious, she gave me a complex about it." I laughed, for it seemed strange to me.

Inside it was bright with people and chatter. I was just deciding what to have to drink when a voice behind me cried: **Leo!** Fancy seeing you here! I turned round to see a petite and very pretty woman with slanting green eyes and pointed chin. She gripped his arm eagerly. I was introduced.

"Well, well. Meet Esme. A great friend of mine." She hung on to his arm, smiling with pleasure at seeing him, curious to know who I was. When he told her I was an actress she exclaimed:

"How thrilling! I adore the theatre." She called over to someone at the bar, trying to make herself heard above the chatter of voices. "You must meet Dick," she said, "He's my husband, on leave from the Merchant Navy. He'll be thrilled to see Leo in a pub. This is the only one I'm allowed in. I'm banned from the others because I say what I think, don't I Leo?"

He looked at her with mock severity. "Now then Esme, I hope you are on your best behaviour. What will you have?" He was trying to edge his way to the bar. She gave a peal of laughter, then in a tragic voice: "Oh Leo, how could you. I'll have another cider." I decided on a port. She linked arms and led me to the window seat. "Isn't he killing? I love him. We're all very proud of our local author. Let's sit over here, there's more room. The men will bring the drinks."

We sat down and she offered me a cigarette. She was strikingly dressed with a crisp long-sleeved shirt that had big turn back cuffs revealing several jangly bracelets. At her neck she wore a pert little red bow-tie and round her tiny waist a large brown belt. Words tumbled out of her.

"Oh I am glad I came here tonight. I've just escaped from my PGs." I must have looked blank for she added, "Paying guests, my dear. I take them all summer and it kills me."

The two men brought the drinks over. Dick turner was pleasant faced, somewhat stockily built with receding hair. He seemed rather over shadowed by his bubbly wife. She chattered on:

"That fish you brought me was delicious Leo. I cooked it in wine." She beamed at him. "He caught it himself."

"By jove, I was lucky that afternoon" he told her, "I got in among them. There were any amount at the harbour mouth."

To me he said. "You look as though you might be hungry, can I get you a sandwich?"

I was starving but a crazy shyness made me hesitate. He got up and went over to the bar, returning presently with a plate of sandwiches.

"Try one."

"Been out on the water much?" asked Dick.

"I've wanted to but we've all been too busy learning lines. I've just been telling Mr. Walmsley about it."

"Call me Leo honey, everyone does." He began to relate my adventures to his friends. They listened in fascinated horror. Esme said she would go raving mad if she had to study like that.

"I was in a nerve hospital once," she said, "but I fell madly in love with a male nurse and they chucked me out."

This broke her up and she spilt most of her drink. When she had recovered she announced that she would round up all her friends and come to see our plays, PGs too.

Suddenly her mood changed from sparkling gaiety to mock despair. She appealed to her friend: "Leo dear, do come along soon and meet this couple I've got. They come from Scunthorpe and they're ghastly."

He chuckled delightedly. "How long are you saddled with them?"

"For another fortnight and they're driving me balmy. If only they would go out more, but they sit around glumly, hardly speaking. They're engaged but they look as miserable as hell. Perhaps you could take them fishing."

He wouldn't commit himself. He was in the middle of a new novel and didn't want any distractions.

"I came out this evening," he said, "because I feel a sympathy with these actors, and because of my darling daughter Ann."

Just then a couple who had come in greeted Leo. The man was tall, slim, in bohemian clothes and with a face so striking and individual that he looked more like an actor than my fellow thespians did. The girl was lovely, with a serene face and a charming diffidence when she asked, could they join us.

"Well well, what a nice surprise," said Leo. "Bob and Joyce, my dear friends. Sit down. Let's get some chairs." The young man fetched a couple. They knew Esme and Dick. They were going on to a dance at one of the sailing clubs. After a short discussion it was agreed that we should all go together and make a night of it.

It didn't take long to reach the club which was near the post office at the end of a narrow lane. As we drew near I heard the strains of dance music. We went up a flight of stairs leading to a spacious room, smoky, full of people. Adjoining this to the left was a smaller one where light refreshments were served at the bar. Nautical pictures, mostly of sailing craft, decorated the walls of the large room which extended at the far end to a balcony over-looking the river.

The floor was packed with dancers. Some people, hoping for partners, sat in easy or hard-backed chairs around the room; dancing alone wasn't in fashion then. The atmosphere was friendly. I hoped I would be staying on at Fowey.

I had many dances, with Leo, and Dick and with fresh faced eager sailing types who said "Oh I say, frightfully sorry" if they trod on my toes. Nice, decent chaps, their conversation peppered with 'jolly good show' and 'ectually'. Among themselves there was a lot of 'in talk' about the foresail and 'tacking to windward.' Some of them were in little groups, talking loudly with strangulated upper crust accents, hoping to impress the outsider. Half grasped, meaningless words came at me as I passed: "came charging down to number three gib....had four rolls in the main..."

I danced with the actor-faced man who was light and easy on his feet as well as mine. He wanted to know all about the repertory company and how long we were staying. He would love to join an outfit like ours, he said.

"I should think you'd be an asset," I told him. Some couples had wandered on to the balcony, where it was cool and romantic. It struck me that here was a perfect stage setting.

"With those french windows leading out, I can almost see the juvenile lead coming on with a sort of romping walk."

He gave a high pitched laugh. "How about me for the juvenile lead?" he asked, with a good deal of self mockery, "Do you think I could say a few lines? I'd have to get my hair cut wouldn't I, and wear white flannels?"

"And one of those striped blazers."

"Like they wore in the old drawing-room comedies." He warmed to the idea and started to clown, and take off the acting of the thirties:

"I say, anyone for tennis?"

****

It was nearly time to go home. The young couple had already left in their Austin Seven car. Esme was just off too. She came over to me. "I've got to dash back now to those dreadful PGs. God knows what they might be doing on my settee!"

The floor was less crowded now. A few couples were dancing to the music from **South Pacific**. The singer's voice was deep and beguiling. "Some enchanted evening......you may meet your true love......you may hear her call you.....across the crowded floor..."

"What a lovely song" said Leo, who hadn't heard it before. We stayed to listen. Then, when the record came to an end "And what a lovely evening. Thank you Stephanie, for coming out with me and making me so happy."

He walked back to my digs with me, along the quiet street.

"I'll know the verdict tomorrow" I said gloomily.

"What verdict?"

"Well, we've got this meeting in the morning to discuss things. I think Tony might decide to cut his losses and push off somewhere else."

"Oh no! You can't go yet. He may give it another week. You may get better houses."

"I do hope so for I love it here. I enjoyed the dance and your friends are fun."

"I'm coming over tomorrow afternoon" Leo said, "so if you would like to go in the boat we could pull up the creek to my place and have tea."

I hesitated. Maybe I felt uncertain about venturing up a lonely creek with someone I hardly knew. "That's awfully nice of you..." I began.

"Look" he said, very kindly, "in case you're wondering about my intentions I must tell you that I'm a decent man."

Now I felt awful about my thoughts and the way he had read them.

We got to the door. I fumbled for my key. He was looking at me with that slightly amused expression. Again he came to the rescue for he laughed and pressed my shoulder.

"I tell you what. Bring along some of your pals. I can take three comfortably."

He must have thought I saw him as a kind of half-crazed seducer. I faced him, then smiled. "I should just love to go in the boat with you, so would Doreen. Joe too probably, if you're sure it won't be too much."

We arranged he would meet the three of us the following day. If plans were changed and we had to leave Fowey, I would leave a message with one of the boatmen. Otherwise he would collect us at four o'clock.

****

CHAPTER VI.

FISHERMAN AUTHOR.

My sense of foreboding was right. The next morning at the Town Hall, Tony gave us our marching orders. We were to move to a village called Dingle, some twelve miles away, set in the heart of the china clay country. We must be packed and ready to leave by eleven a.m. on Monday.

"I feel so sad" I told Doreen, when the meeting was over. "I suppose we'll never come back."

"Oh why do we have to go?" she said, child-like, catching my mood. The rest of the company didn't seem to care one way or another. Then Joe reassured us by pointing out that twelve miles wasn't so far and we didn't give a show on Sundays did we? My spirits brightened then, and we all looked forward to the trip in the boat.

That afternoon, Leo was waiting for us in his dinghy at the Town Quay. She was a sturdy looking boat, painted navy blue and grey with touches of scarlet. He unfastened the painter and brought her alongside the steps. He was wearing his fisherman's togs, sea boots and corduroys. There was a fishing rod and two lines in the boat.

One of the locals called out, "Any fish about Leo?" He called back cheerily and we all got in, taking care to avoid treading in a tray of wriggling live bait. Doreen and I were told to sit astern, Joe to go forrit.

"You go aft, because you're daft" she told him. It was a great giggle to her. She shrieked as she stepped into the boat and it lurched a bit. She shrieked again when she sat right down on a large wet worm.

Rowing appeared as natural to Leo as walking. With strong even strokes he made the boat glide across the harbour. It was a beautiful sight with all the sailing boats on the very blue water. There was not much wind to help them along, just a pleasant breeze.

We were now approaching the scene I had first admired from the Quay. We passed a jutting bit of headland and were now at the mouth of Pont Creek. Leo slowed down and rested on the oars for a bit. "Isn't it superb?" he said. The water was shining and transparent. Rising on both sides of the creek was this high land like a Norwegian fiord. There were wild flowers on the banks, black-thorn, mimosa, pink campion. What a place to live, I thought, surrounded by such beauty.

Suddenly Leo became very excited, saying he could see a shoal of fish swimming by. "By God I can see them!" he shouted, "Quick hand me the line!" We found it for him. "Can one of you take over?" he asked. I was longing to, I had done a spot of rowing on the Norfolk Broads as a child. We changed places. I started rowing slowly round the buoy that was anchored at the head of the creek, following Leo's instructions as he began to pay out his line.

"We ought to get a bite soon" he said. I felt wonderfully alive, and at the same time peaceful and serene. Here was a feeling of timelessness; no rush or bother; no noisy cars.

Lewis Carroll had written a verse about being on the water:

"A boat beneath a sunny sky." I thought of his lovely introduction to Alice In Wonderland:

> "All in the golden afternoon
> Full leisurely we glide..."

I went on pulling round the buoy. Then a shout from Leo brought me back to earth. "Hoy! I've got a bite! Pull the oars in, now ship them. Be ready with the net Joe. Good God, I think its a big one!" He was standing up with his back to me, pulling in his line. As he got to the end of the line I could see plainly the fish just under the surface of the water, swimming frantically from side to side. Leo was wildly excited.

"It's a bass!" he yelled. He swung it over the boat where it fell on to the seat, gasping and flapping about. "My God, it's very seldom I get a fish like that. I usually have to set the net. And bass don't usually take ragworm either."

The poor fish was flapping so violently it sometimes leapt right up in the air. "It will soon be dead" he assured me. "I'll give it a whack on the head in a minute." He asked me to turn around and pull back to the place where he had got the bite, as clearly we were in among them. I went on pulling for a bit while he called out, "A litle on your left, now pull hard on your right." But we didn't have the same luck twice.

"One more try," said Leo, "here goes." He put another squirming worm onto the hook, ignoring Doreen's audible groans, and flung the line overboard. Still no more bites; the fish must have sensed danger. But I think Leo would have been happy to go on angling for the rest of the day.

After a while he hauled in the line and told me to carry on. He was still very excited about the bass. "I wish I could send it to my boy, but it wouldn't arrive fresh. I'll make a cast of it for him."

We were nearing a little cove that had a slipway leading up to a cottage with a rust coloured roof. This must be it, I thought, and slowed down to admire it.

"We're not there yet" said Leo, "Go on a bit more, it's round the bend."

"Like you" said Doreen (she meant me).

We were approaching it now. I pulled hard on my right oar, and we turned in "Here we are" said Leo. Looking over my shoulder I saw that we had come to a larger cove. Beyond this, at the top of a path, sheltered in a valley, was a dark, almost black, army style wooden hut. I felt a pang of disappointment. The cottage had looked so appealing.

The boat grounded. We all jumped out and Leo made fast to a line he called a frape. There were two pulleys which were fixed at either end, and once secured to the rope, the boat could be hauled in or out.

A sleek black cat hurried down the path. It leapt straight into the boat, scenting out the fish. A shout from Leo sent it leaping out again. "No you don't you devil." He quickly seizes his prize, hooking his fingers into its gill. "You'll have to wait" he told the cat, "I'll go out later and get a fish for you Choo-i. Come and say hello to our visitors." We all stroked and made a fuss of him.

Then with Choo-i leading the way, and a lovely smell of honey-suckle coming from the rocky cliff above, we went up two flights of steps to the path. I forgot my earlier disappointment that the hut wasn't the cottage when I saw the rambler roses growing up against the walls and some giant sunflowers. Outside the hut, at the top of some steps, was a wooden balcony. A large fish net was draped over one end. The hut was raised on piles, as the land sloped down towards the cove. There was a lawn to the right of the path, and running parallel, a fresh water stream. Doreen went up to it and found water cress growing there.

I went over to the sunflowers. Some were taller than me, coming above my head. They looked almost human. "Come on up." Leo was already on the balcony. I went up the wooden staircase. He pushed open the front door. "I tidied the place this morning, it was in an awful mess."

I went in and saw a large room with water colour paintings all round the walls. There were several windows, one very large overlooking the front with a glorious view of the creek. By this window was a table with a typewriter on it and several pages of manuscript.

"What do you think of it? Come and look at the view." I went over to the table. I could see down the path to the water where the blue boat looked happy on her moorings; and across the creek to the high land.

"It's heavenly.... like a dream."

"I never tire of it, there's always something to see. At low tide it's fascinating to watch the gulls and oyster catchers....the heron too, he hunts flat fish. Like a beautiful picture, it goes on giving."

"It's so peaceful, so still." The others joined us. Both exclaimed on the size of the room.

"It's so big! You'd never think so from the outside."

"Who did the paintings?"

"Come and look over here."

At the opposite end of the room with a view was an ancient chinese cabinet, and next to it some white bookshelves, heavily stacked with books. There were African carvings and pots along the top shelf. I looked at the paintings.

"Who did these?"

"I did. I don't know if they're any good though. I got a terrific craze for painting a few years ago. A sort of painting fever. I quite like that one over there." He pointed to a picture of Whitby Harbour, very delicately done in pastel colours. It was alive and made you feel you were right there. All the paintings were studies of scenery; seascape and landscape. They were quite individual and full of feeling. One was particularly striking which was called 'The Lignum Vitae Tree, Curacao.'

"How do you like my chair?" said Leo, he was referring to one near the cabinet. It had a charming, unusual shape, the back being completely round and smooth. "I made it myself from a pair of ship's bellows.....Come on I'll show you the rest of the place then we'll have tea." We followed him through a door, left of the cabinet, which led into a small passage with two rooms either side; one was his bedroom, and viewing was strictly prohibited— it hadn't been swept for ages! The other was a bathroom just big enough to hold a bath, wash basin and airing cupboard. Then up four steps through another door. We were inside a huge bright kitchen with windows at either end. There was a family size table against the wall near the door, chunky, thick and as homemade as marmalade, with a cream top and legs coloured scarlet. Garden style canvas backed chairs were ranged round it. A cooking stove on a marble table top stood near the window overlooking the lawn, and at the other end of the room, a sink and a wooden draining board.

The whole place was totally different from anything I had seen before, with the possible exception of a log cabin or a Swiss chalet. Apart from a big Chinese carpet in the front room, and some rugs, the floors were bare, painted with liquid linoleum. Just the essentials, I thought; no fuss or bother with table cloths or frilly curtains, yet how attractive were those framing the front room windows. They were rust coloured, made out of sail cloth.

"I made all these," said Leo, indicating the shelves which held bright crockery, and a big cupboard where he kept his provisions. "Mostly from driftwood. It's surprising what I find washed up on the cove after a storm." I looked at them, gaily painted with the same touches of scarlet on a background of cream or light blue, liking everything I saw, the chunky table, the oil lamp hanging from the ceiling, the blue and white striped mugs on the shelves. Friendly, honest, real. There was no pretension.

Peace was here. And love.

Such a lot of love must have gone into the making of this home. I wanted to tell him so. He was leaning against a big chest under the cupboard, rolling himself a cigarette, pressing the tobacco in, firming it down with his thumb. He had nice big hands, masculine, rough with square shaped fingers. The sun was streaming through the window on to his face; it was heavily lined, strong. The lines giving dignity. You could tell that he had lived, and been through it too. Was he lonely sometimes?

"What's through that door?" Doreen was referring to yet another one next to the cupboard.

Leo had lit his cigarette, first apologising for it. Doreen made a wry face, so did Joe. It was herbal tobacco. I found it quite intoxicating, mysterious as incense with something clean and woodland about it, forever to be stamped in my memory of that summer afternoon in July.

On we went again, following our guide through the fourth door and into a passage with two rooms at either side. All except one, which was virtually empty save for a chair and some odds and ends, were the bedrooms. They had nice big old-fashioned beds with thick army blankets and dressing tables and chests of drawers of the 1910 period. Most of the furniture, like the wardrobes and bedside tables, were home-made. Here again, no carpets, just liquid lino, dark blue here, rust red there, and some rugs. Above each bed, fixed to the wall was, an Aladdin oil lamp. The room nearest the end of the hut had a port-hole window in the door.

At the end of the passage, the last door led us out to a path which curved to the right joining the one in front. Opposite this was a patch of lawn, slightly unkempt. We turned left, passing a bush covered with white and mauve lilac and came to a vegetable garden, well stocked with runner beans, spinach, lettuce, and potatoes. Beyond this were apple, pear and plum trees laden with fruit. We were invited to pick some and then we came round to the front of the hut and went indoors for tea.

Leo filled the kettle. "All my water comes from the stream," he told us. "I pump it."

"But how?" I wanted to know. The explanation was a three and a half horse-power petrol engine with centrifugal pump. This went over my head a bit so I said nothing, just quietly marvelled at water coming fresh from a stream.

"It lifts up to forty feet," he told Joe, "and goes into a tank supplying the kitchen and bathroom." A bit more talk about engines -Joe had a motor bike - then Doreen said could she do anything to help, which really meant that she was starving and hurry up with the tea.

Leo put the blue and white mugs on the table, with the matching sugar bowl and milk jug. All the time he was talking. Not many people could lead his sort of life, away from shops and pubs, and how he would hate having neighbours, the noise of a town. He filled the tea-pot then went to the cupboard and took out a jam roll. He put it on a huge dinner plate and plonked them all down on the table.

We drew up our chairs. Suddenly he turned his back on us. "I can't pour out. I get self-conscious." He turned to me. "You do it." Another glimpse of his character. This was the pub bit again. I took over while Doreen stared at the jam roll. It looked lonely on the vast plate.

"Help yourselves, there's a knife in the drawer." We didn't need coaxing.

"I'm in a state of nerves," Leo said, now joining us at the table, "wondering if this friend can help me with my boy."

"How old is Shawn?" I handed him a mug of tea.

"He's eight. He's a lovely boy. You'll fall for him. It's ironic because I'm perfectly capable of looking after my own son.... he's dark like his mother." He looked round at us. "I've been through hell. There's not the slightest doubt about that. But in spite of everything, I'm still in love with her."

Joe stirred his tea and Doreen loked subdued.

In those days I was care-free knowing only the lighter side of life, untouched by sadness. So when I murmured "How awful, you must be lonely" it was more in token sympathy. I had yet to live.

"Yes, I've been very lonely since she packed up on me. Sometimes on dark winter nights when you can't hear a sound, I've come pretty close to despair....but it's always having plenty to do that has kept me going. I lead a very active life; the boat is my one form of transport, and there's the garden. But most important of all is the book I'm writing. I'm trying to make a come-back. It's a sequel to **Love In The Sun**."

"That's the story of how you came to Fowey and found the hut isn't it?"

"Yes, by God, and rented it for only three bob a week. What a press that book had. The critics raved over it. One described it as 'A little Eden in Cornwall' while another likened it to Robinson Crusoe. I came very near to making a fortune with that book. It was a best-seller, all set to be made into a film in Hollywood. Then the war came and killed it off."

We were all keen to read this book. He told us it was out of print but he had a few copies and would lend us one. We thanked him, then Joe asked what the sequel was about and if it was nearly completed.

"Good Lord no, I've only done three chapters but I'm confident it will be one of my best books. I'm calling it **The Golden Waterwheel**."

"I like that," I said, "it sounds lyrical."

"Tell us what it's about," said Doreen.

"Well I always dreamt of having a waterwheel and breeding trout. This book describes finding a derelict estate in Yorkshire between the moors and the sea, with forty two acres of land and a babbling stream running through. I was able to buy the land having sold the film rights of one of my books."

"Oh,so you did have one of your books made into a film?"

"Yes, but that's another story. No, to get back to this one, I'm describing the adventures of building a home, the joy and excitement of it, reclaiming the land, breeding trout. What a place it was."

"It sounds like a dream home, I don't think I would have wanted to leave it," said Doreen, "But were you sorry to leave Fowey?"

"Yes very. It was a real wrench. But we needed something bigger with our family increasing."

"Like me, you come from the north don't you?" said Joe.

"Yes, I was brought up in Robin Hood's Bay. Dad was the local artist. There was plenty of inspiration for him there and he did some fine water colours."

Some chat then with Joe and Doreen about Liverpool, their home town. Leo told them his family had come from there.

I was curious to know what had brought him back to Fowey. "We had to leave our home which we called 'Adder Howe'. The war was in its second year and the moor became an artillery range and battle ground and the beaches were all closed. We ploughed up some of our land to grow food, and found, under the soil, a bed of ganister. This was needed for the war effort. So we had to go."

"How awful! All the work you put into it. Did you come straight back here?"

"No, not directly."

"Don't leave us in suspense. Where did you go after you were chucked out?" Leo looked at the three of us sitting round the table and smiled.

"It's nice to be chatting to you like this. I mustn't get too carried away though."

"Just tell us what happened."

"Well, I sold Adder Howe and we moved to Pembrokeshire. I bought a very large house, a beautiful place, designed by John Nash. But it needed a lot of work on it, being more or less derelict. I gave up writing for a bit and became a farmer, for the land had to be re-claimed. I also did carpentry and bricklaying and we kept hens. My wife ran the place as a nursery boarding school and we took in evacuees."

"No wonder you had to give up writing."

"Well, I couldn't tell which were my own kids sometimes, there were so many of them in the house."

"My father would have gone mad," I said. He laughed at this, picturing the horror of Nat. Gubbins being surrounded by 'Awful children.'

"I think I might have qualified for saint -hood in those days. However it all went well at first, with ploughing and sowing, we got a good crop of oats. But once the air raids were over the evacuees returned to London and our pupils began falling off. Things went from bad to worse, for after ploughing and sowing the remaining fields I found they were contaminated with a parasitic fungus. The whole lot had to be burnt. I lost all the money I'd spent on the land. We were in a dreadful fix, financially. I was in the red you see. And then our marriage broke up." He got up and went over to the window. "My nerves were in a bad state at the time...but here, I'm talking too much."

"Please go on," I said.

He rejoined us at the table.

"After that I sold Temple Druid, our Welsh home and returned here. I had alterations done and worked on the garden to make it ship shape for the children's holidays. I look forward each year to that.

We were silent for a while. Leo pushed the rest of the jam roll towards us.

"Now let's get back to you and your plays, and come to that my own play **Sally Lunn**. I should love to see it performed again."

Would we be able to put it on? we asked him.

"It's difficult to stage, especially in a town hall. You can tell your producer he can have a shot at it if he likes."

This was really kind as Tony was always on the lookout for plays.

It was pleasant sitting in the sunny kitchen. We discussed the idea of producing **Sally Lunn**, the casting, and the scenery. For the latter it would be a case of make do as we only carried two sets. Leo rolled me a cigarette. I took one puff. It had a strange but agreeable flavour.

"If she's playing **Sally** what part would I have?" asked Doreen.

"You could be **Amy**, her sister-in -law."

"And you," I told Leo, "could come to rehearsals and give advice."

"Don't forget" said Joe, "we're packing up tomorrow."

For a moment I had forgotten. Now the thought hung like a cloud over the bright afternoon. Leo came up with a practical suggestion. Wouldn't Lostwithiel be a good proposition for Howard Productions? If we got a good run there it might lead back to Fowey. He didn't think there was a cinema there nor did he know the size of the population.

"But you couldn't get a worse house than last night." He chuckled at the memory of an audience of six. "It's ironic I should find myself sitting behind a clergyman. I have an antipathy towards vicars. Catholicism is my pet aversion." With perhaps an inner sense he asked Joe if he had a faith.

"I'm a Catholic," Joe answered quietly.

"I thought as much!" He looked at Joe quizzically as though trying to read his mind. "Can you honestly tell me you accept their dogma? Their diabolic conception of hell-fire?" Joe wouldn't be drawn.

"I've no patience whatever with the supernatural, nor with stupidity." Leo was looking at me now. I didn't want to be thought stupid so I said quickly, "I was a Catholic once, when I was small. But not anymore. I haven't been to church for ages so they must have rejected me."

"Good. Some of it must have sunk in though," he said gloomily. "They get at your mind, especially if they catch you young."

Doreen changed the subject by asking for more tea. I poured some out for her.

"No, there's only one religion for me," Leo went on, "and that's humanism." No one pressed for details and the conversation switched back to plays.

Suddenly Leo remembered that the tide was ebbing. His boat would be going aground. He got up and hurried down to the cove. We followed him, Doreen singing, happy with a bag of fruit she had picked, Joe with his thoughtful silence. I turned to have a last look. I thought 'May-be I'll come back here one day.'

The heat had gone from the sun but it was still shining; the creek was calm and smooth as polished glass. Leo untied the dinghy. She was afloat.

We all got in and just then a family of swans glided by, breaking the sleepy stillness of the water.

****

CHAPTER VII.

VILLAGE CHILD FOR SIXPENCE.

We were in the van, the whole lot of us, just pulling out of Fowey and heading for the village of Dingle.

It was hard leaving the little sea-port which looked lovelier than ever that morning.

We sat where we could, jostled against the props and scenery, swaying where the narrow road curved sharply right or left.

In those days there were no government subsidies or hand-outs for repertory companies. You had to sink or swim, and we were sinking fast. The takings of the box office had proved inadequate for us to receive our share, and there was no prospect of being paid until the end of the week when it was hoped we might have got better houses.

Old Mrs. Howard sat hunched up on one of the big prop baskets. Her skirt was long, not far from the floor and round her head and shoulders was a woollen shawl. The expression in those dim eyes was cynical, one who had been there and back and hadn't liked it very much either. I wondered just how many bumpety, jogging, lurching journeys in the van she must have made in this hand-to-mouth roughing it life. Had she ever slept between silk sheets, felt proud and hailed a taxi; soaked in a hot bath of scented water?

"Fancy wearing a shawl when it's so hot" whispered Doreen who sported shorts and a sleeveless top.

"She feels the cold" I suggested. It was one thing to rough it at seventeen, but when you're seventy plus, that's really rough.

The journey wasn't long, about an hour, and when we arrived we pulled up at another town hall. We all had to lend a hand un-loading the props. That night we were doing **Freda** again. Doreen and I would have to go over our scene many times if we didn't want a repeat of the monumental dry. But first we must go digs hunting, a risky kind of sport where you couldn't always win, and it was best to start early.

Having pulled our weight, we set off armed with merriment and Mars bars.

There was little charm about Dingle; it was larger than a village, with a few ordinary looking shops, a post office and some rather ugly houses and bungalows with names like 'Lamorna', 'Rosevilla', and 'Bellevue'. We t ramped around knocking at doors, ringing bells. Curtains twitched as we passed and curious eyes peered out. We got glimpses of Aspidistra plants and china ornaments. We weren't a bit shy. It was all a great giggle. Stout pinafored ladies came to the door, some flushed from the wash, others embarrassed, wishing they could help. Some had wary expressions and a cigarette between their lips. They opened the door cagily and said they would ask their husbands later. But some were kind and asked us in, and one lady made coffee for us. She seemed to enjoy bringing out the best china, and to our speechless joy, the silver biscuit barrel.

While we bit into the custard creams we complimented her on her family photographs. I imagined there would be many front parlours like this one, with protective linen covers over the chair backs, china displayed in glass fronted cupboards, and potted plants.

It was nearing the afternoon before we found a place, a bungalow called 'Cosy Nook'. It was set a little way from the other houses, nearer the open country, and there was a field behind.

A short fat lady answered our knock. She had rather wild staring eyes but her manner was pleasant. She already had three other guests so it might be a bit of a squash, but she never liked to turn anyone away. We could have her room. Would that be putting her out? No, not really for she was used to that, besides 'we're in this world to help each other aren't we?' (that old line, I thought) and now if we would follow her with our cases...

The room was crammed full with her belongings, clothes strewn over chairs, boxes bulging under beds. But it wouldn't take her long, she said, to get it straight. We hadn't seen a Cafe in our search for digs, so we decided to take a chance on the Box Office and settle for full board which our landlady could give us at reasonable terms. She went off to see about lunch, first telling us her name was Mrs. Batts, we could call her Ruby if we liked.

"I don't think I do like" I said after she had gone. There were two single beds with a small table between. I 'bagged' the one nearest the wall, a throw back to childhood days, it seemed cosier. We felt the mattresss. Not too bad. On the wall above the bed were slogans. Doreen read out:

"GO OFTEN TO THE HOUSE OF GOD, WEEDS CHOKE THE UNUSED PATH".

"Oh dear, she's one of those!"

"Look at this one, 'THE LORD WILL PROVIDE'"

"I hope that doesn't take care of our lunch."

It didn't, but there was a disconcertingly long wait between grilled fish and cold rhubarb while Mrs. Batts went out and belted out hymns at the piano. Finally we escaped from her to the field, as she was over fond of talking, and we had to work hard at our scene before rehearsing in the hall. They had set the stage just like it was that first night in Fowey; the memory of it sent a shiver of fright through me. But we weren't going to dry up again.

Happily all went well that night. It seemed that the whole village had turned out to see us. If we fluffed a little now and then so did the rest of the cast, who knew the play better than us. The main thing was, the audience liked us, and this looked promising for the rest of the week.

Back in our digs that night we unpacked the rest of our things. Once again we were to breathe a sigh of relief that the play was off our minds. Tomorrow it would be **Wuthering Heights**, the mixture as before, but it was uncertain if Tony would risk "**Love on the Dole**" again.

Before leaving, Leo had given me a Penguin edition of his novel **Foreigners**. He had also lent us a copy of **Love in the Sun**.

In bed that night I picked up the Penguin book that was on the table beside me, and not for the first time I turned it over to admire the photo of the author on the back cover. It was taken by the 'Yorkshire Post'. All that was best in his face had been captured. The expression in his eyes, the compassion, it was all there. Underneath the photo there was a piece about him and his literary output. It began by stating that in World War I he had served in East Africa and had been awarded the M.C.

"Leo must have been terribly brave" I said to Doreen, reading it out to her: "He has been on many scientific expeditions in Central Africa, experiences which have formed the exotic background to several of his books. Knows intimately the life of fishermen, about which he writes with such sympathy and sense of exhilaration in '**Three Fevers**'. Ah look! Now it mentions Fowey. From the Yorkshire coast he went with his wife to Cornwall where they made a home from a derelict hut and their furniture from washed up planks. Here '**Foreigners**' was written and later his fascinating and beautiful '**Love in the Sun**'."

"I'm looking forward to reading that".

It had been a pleasant surprise to learn from Leo when he took me home from the dance that night, that Esme lived next door to my digs. I had called on her the following morning and she had given me and Doreen an invitation to stay with her any time we liked.

With this happy prospect in mind I opened the book and began to read.

At first things weren't too bad at 'Cosy Nook'. When we were not studying like maniacs we played the piano and sang duets, sometimes joined by the three other guests, all male, who were china clay workers. We found ways of dodging Mrs. Batts, for we were all a little uneasy about her, and the over-brightness of her eyes.

Wuthering Heights had gone down very well, every seat had been taken. It was good to feel that we were becoming popular. The next night we were to do a different play and I had the lead. The play was called **While Parents Sleep**.

"You know it's a pity" said Doreen, "that Mr Walmsley wasn't able to see **Wuthering Heights** when we did it at Fowey."

"Yes, even though I had a very small part."

"Well you'll make up for it tonight" she said with certain relish, "for you're on most of the time."

Before she had time to gloat any further about me having the hard slog for a change, I gently put her wise.

"Isn't it a wonderful coincidence" I said sweetly, "that I should have played this part quite recently in my previous repertory company." My part as **Bubbles** was a very lively one in a jolly, bubbly comedy.

"As long as you're happy" said Doreen, starting to giggle "and heven't forgotten that there's a scene where you have to sit on the leading man's lap and be very coy."

"Oh! I *had* forgotten."

"And not only that" Doreen went on,when she could speak for laughing. "The leading man is ——— you've guessed it. Tony."

"Oh NO!"

"And you've got some daft lines to say like 'ooh you are awful.... I promised ma I'd be home by ten."

I didn't mind about the lines. But I didn't relish the thought of sitting on Tony's lap.

"I really am glad" said Doreen smugly, "that in this play I only have a small part."

On the morning of the play, Doreen and I were sitting in the front room about to have breakfast, when, looking up, I saw my blue blouse and skirt coming in with the porridge. Too stunned to speak, I watched while the plates were set before us. "Tea be in directly" said Mrs. Batts, making for the door. I stared after her in fascinated horror.

"WELL! Can you beat that? She's wearing MY CLOTHES! My blouse and skirt."

"I thought I recognised the blouse....".

"AND the skirt. She is really....".

"It wouldn't be coincidence? She may have some like yours."

"No they're mine, I know my clothes, besides they don't fit her. What a cheek!."

"She must have nipped in very quickly and tried them on because we haven't been out of the room long."

"That funny glitter in her eye....I never did like...."

"SSHH she's coming back."

With the innocent look of a child having raided the cake tin Mrs.Batts came in humming with the tea and toast.

"Why on earth didn't you say something?" asked Doreen after she'd gone.

"I can't until I have had a look in the wardrobe to make sure, although I'm certain those clothes are mine. She's mad you know. Just our luck to get saddled with a maniac."

"Cleptomaniac you mean."

After breakfast we rushed along to the bedroom. There was my blouse and skirt hanging up, not in the wardrobe but on the door. "She must have been a quick change artist at one time, that's all I can say," said Doreen.

We spent the morning in the field, me revising my part, Doreen learning hers, which didn't take long. Shortly before lunch, having learnt her lines she went to the village to buy some things.

It was nice in the field, sitting on a rug. There was little studying to do as I remembered the part quite well. I decided to make allowances for Mrs. Batts. She had been kind to take us in. It was probably only a little lapse, or she was a trifle eccentric, even thinking in her crazed way, that the clothes were hers as they were in her wardrobe. It wouldn't happen again.

Just then Doreen burst in on my charitable thoughts.

"Guess what! You'll never believe....I've just seen my pink dress coming out of the post office!"

"WHAT!"

"It's true. I was choosing cards when I happened to look up and saw Mrs. Batts coming away from the counter."

"Did she see you?"

"Yes, and spoke to me. She said 'This dress suits me m'dear don't it?' and went out. You needn't laugh. It's my best one."

"I can't help it....Oh Doreen, I said she was nuts."

Doreen was beginning to laugh now. She flopped down on her heels.

"If you could have seen how....how absolutely RIDICULOUS...."

"Don't," I said weakly. "My sides ache."

"How ridiculous she looked, being so fat....in that three tiered skirt." We were falling about now. "And her enormous hips stretching it to its very limit."

When we had finally recovered, Doreen sat up and became practical. There was only one thing for it, she said, we must take all our clothes to the hall and leave them there otherwise we'll end up by going batty as well.

"We will if we stay there much longer" I said, grimly.

But we did stay on. There was little alternative as we were now being bombarded with an ever increasing number of plays to learn, so there was not time to search for new digs. Doreen tried to get a key for our room as she heard that Mrs. Batts walked in her sleep and it scared her. But she was unlucky. Mrs. Batts didn't hold with doors being locked, not even the bathroom and loo (an embarrassing truth we had already discovered).

While Parent Sleep was very popular. We played to a large audience which chuckled happily throughout the performance. Television wasn't in everyone's home then and it was as much a social event to come to our plays, where everyone knew each other as well as a way of killing time. It was a thrill to hear the audience laugh when I said my lines, or introduced my own bits of comedy. I had experienced this response when I had played the part before. It was re-assuring for we got no praise or encouragement from our producer, but plenty of blame if we weren't quick on his cues, or did anything that might show him in an unfavourable light.

Mrs. Batts came to see the play, wearing her own clothes for a change, and enjoyed it. "You did a proper job there girls" she told us afterwards.

From now on it was all hard work. Having proved popular at Dingle we were going to stay on, learning new plays. If the box office had been bad we would have moved on doing repeats.

The plays were various and included: **Night Must Fall, They Walk Alone, Random Harvest, The Winslow Boy, Peg O' My Heart, Hatters Castle, Jane Eyre, This Happy Breed** and many more. With a few exceptions they were all fine plays. The ones that weren't were usually so dreadfully funny that it was hard to make them sound credible. For instance, coming straight after **'Parents Sleep'** we had an antiquated Victorian relic called **'Lady Audley's Secret'**. Apart from not knowing what her secret was, the daughter appears to have swallowed a dictionary in this scene I had with Jimmy. This was how my part was written out.

Daughter "I knew it, I knew it. Oh Papa isn't it shameful of him."
(Cue from Papa)..."prevent you ever speaking to him"
(Crosses left)
Daughter (weeping) "Oh the false, deceitful, perfidious, perjured profligate."
Papa...."Forget the base fellow, forget him."
Daughter "I will, I will, Oh the artful crocodile."   (Exits left).

To add to the hilarity of acting in plays like this, they often had asides where the actor speaks confidently to his audience behind his hand, in this fashion:

"Let us follow the others."
Robert..."hope you are well Lady Audley."
Lady Audley..."Quite well thank you (aside) "he is too evil by half."
Robert..."me take your coat."
Lady Audley..."Thank you" (aside) "I do not like him being so familiar."

We did quite a few Victorian plays, mostly melodramas, including **The Bells** and a weird Manx play called **The Rosary** where Doreen played a crazed Nun, forced to take a vow of silence, who is finally banished forever after a man is seen leaving her bedroom.

Most of our days now, and nights too, were spent learning one part after another. There was hardly time even for meals. We became desperate, giddy, dizzy and hysterical by turns, often not knowing which play we were acting in at the time.

Our producer had nice ways of surprising his actors; like giving out a song to be learnt half an hour before the curtain rose, and once, when I was on the stage ready to play a scene with him, he suddenly started crawling and lurching before me with a paralysed arm and twisted face. This was a horrific shock because he had read the part quite straight at rehearsal.

If we three newcomers to the company were kept in constant suspense with Tony like a magician pulling plays out of a hat, his old mother was a puppet dancing to his strings. This gallant old trouper had numerous roles to play both on and off stage, for she combined the duties of prompter, wardrobe mistress, box office attendant, cooker of fry-ups in the van, scene shifter..."come on, all lend a hand, you too mother...PUSH!" and understudy. Besides this she had to be ready to perform any part her son demanded of her: one night a gracious lady pouring tea for her friends with a trembling hand...the next, down on her knees with a brush and slopping pail of water, scrubbing the floor in a play called **Over The Hill**. Then as mother in **East Lynne** with a shawl over her head, peering through the window, the snowflakes falling...calling out "Dead!... and never called me mother."

This produced sympathetic murmurs from kind hearted Cornish ladies in the audience, "poor 'ol soul, 'tis a shame, dear of her too."

If there was an excess of characters in a play, Tony roped in the local talent. When he required a child actor there was always a willing candidate and the child would perform for sixpence an hour. This provided extra pathos in a sad play, bringing sniffs from the warm, spontaneous audience. There was one old man of eighty who had been in the regular army and seen lots of action. He came every night to watch us. He had a waxed moustache and was very tall, with bright blue eyes. At first I thought he looked a bit severe, then his wife told me that during the death scene of the child in **East Lynne** tears streamed down his face. "I said 'Get away Dad, 'tis only theatricals', but Dad do dearly love the little children."

A bond had sprung up between us and the people of Dingle. We received invitations to tea, and when we had small parts to learn, which was not often, we sampled their lavish hospitality. The table would be set as though for a birthday or Christmas tea, with Cornish pasties, yeast buns, plates of ham, saffron cake, tinned salmon, jellies, trifles and Cornish cream. We could hardly believe people could be so kind, so generous. When they were able to lure Mrs. Howard away from her duties, they made a special fuss of her, coaxing her into the comfiest chair, plying her with food, and confiding to me:

" I takes off my hat to she, the dear 'ol thing. But I would dearly like to know her had a bed to sleep in."

I woke early on the morning of our second Saturday at Dingle. I sat up and stretched my arms out. My heart felt light with a quiet sort of happiness. Tomorrow, Doreen and I were going to Fowey. We had not been able to make it last week, but on Monday we were doing a play called **Over The Hill** and we had only very small parts in it. We would catch a bus and we would be off to the little sea-port, first calling at Esme's cottage. Then I would look out for that now familiar figure, clad in sea-boots and fisherman's guernsey. He always pulled in to Fowey in the afternoons, I remembered.

Mrs. Howard was the star in Monday's play about a poor old mother, bent double with scrubbing floors and washing crocks, who lives under her son's constant threat of being sent to the workhouse... Over The Hill. In the end her worst fears are realised and she is sent packing...(Over The Hill).

I got up quietly, not to wake Doreen and went along to the bathroom with my towel; humming happily I opened the door and stumbled straight into a figure crouched on its knees with head bent. I gave a gasp of surprise.

"Oh! I'm so sorry." I retreated nervously.

"Won't be a minute," said that now familiar voice of our landlady.

I hesitated, scared that she might ask me to join her on the floor.

Then out came Mrs. Batts looking weird in a purple bath robe.

"I hope I didn't startle you" she said, staring at me rather wildly, "but what with the house being so full, this is the only room where I can pray."

It was awkward to know how to comment on this so I apologised and said I was hoping for a bath, but no hurry.

"Well I've finished now so I'll turn the tap on for you."

She bent to do this, first adding "I always like a little chat with the Lord each morning." Then she stood and faced me.

"I hope you believe in the Lord."

Something told me this was coming, so I was prepared for it.

"Yes I do" I assured her, "I really do... absolutely." This seemed to satisfy her and she went on her way rejoicing.

We were doing **See How They Run** that night. I had my old part of **Ida** the mad maid. It was bully for Doreen too; she had learnt her part after arriving in Fowey.

Tony had secured local talent for the part of a young sergeant who appeared in the third act. At the last moment, the youth who was going to play the part fell and broke his leg. Our producer had to think fast. He looked round us all assembled on the stage... and he didn't hesitate.

"Mother, you're on" he said.

With only an hour to go, the poor old lady had to rapidly learn the part, struggle into full battle dress, tucking all her grey hair under a forage cap, and finally stagger on to the stage with a rifle slung over one shoulder.

Village Child For Sixpence

"It's wicked you know" Joe said to me, as he drew the curtains back.

That night the audience laughed so much at **See How They Run** that we were going to repeat it next week.

Things were looking up. Doreen and I counted out our money after the show. We had now been paid twice.

Tomorrow we would get the bus to Fowey.

****

CHAPTER VIII.

MARMITE ON THE MANTLEPIECE.

Sunlight streaming into the room woke me up. I lay for a while listening to the birds, thinking. What to wear today? My green dress, the grey and white? I settled on a misty blue, the colour of a thunderstorm. I dressed and went into the garden. The air was full of the sweet smell of summer. We had the whole day to ourselves.

It was a job to wake Doreen but I managed it by almost pushing her out of bed, and shortly we were on our way to catch the bus.

It was like coming home to be in Fowey again, to walk down from the bus stop and see a glimpse of blue water, and along the narrow path by the church, with trees on each side. Bells were ringing. People were coming out of the Sunday service. They smiled a friendly good-morning.

There was no answer when we knocked at Esme's cottage, but the window was open so we climbed in. We found her sitting in her flower filled garden by the water's edge. It was like a miniature Venice with the boats going by. She was delighted to see us and got up and made coffee which we carried outside. We could stay the night, she said; feel free to do what we liked.

We stretched out to sunbathe. Leo wouldn't be coming across yet.

By the afternoon the sun was intensely hot. I could feel my face colouring.

"Am I getting tanned?" I asked hopefully. "No just pink" said Esme, which wasn't true. But she reminded me that it was nearly three o'clock, the time Leo would be on the Quay.

"You'd better hurry" she said.

When we got there he was just nearing the steps, standing up in the boat, winding in his fishing line. He had already heard our voices at the edge of the Quay and he looked up and called "HOY" and raised his hand. Then having finished winding in, he picked up an oar and sculled into the steps. We went to meet him. He was smiling with pleasure when he saw us.

"Well, well! So you made it after all —— catch hold of the painter will you —— can you take this?" The latter was an ingenious invention of his own making, a wooden box with partitions to carry six bottles of milk. Doreen took the milk box and I held the painter while he picked up his rucksack and got out. He made to take the rope from me but I wanted to bring the boat round myself. At the railings he confided in sotto voice "God I'm glad you've come. I'm in a hell of a jam; tell you about it later." He showed me how to make fast with a rolling hitch and then collected two pints of milk and the Sunday papers from inside the doorway of the river-side cottage, the one with the dove cote. He had some letters to post and a couple of things to buy. "Take a walk on with me" he said. We left Doreen sitting dangling her feet in the water. As we came away from the Quay he pressed my shoulder warmly.

"You look lovely in that frock" he said, " I'd been hoping like hell you'd be able to come." I felt happy when he said that and I explained why I couldn't come before.

"I looked out for you last Sunday" he said, "I don't mind telling you I was disappointed. I've been working hard on the book, re-writing, cutting. Got another chapter finished. I'm quite pleased with it. Oh, and I've made a plaster cast of that bass for Shawn." Here he paused and looked at me thoughtfully. "I've got a proposition to put to you; I feel a bit awful suggesting it...." again he paused. I wondered what was coming and encouraged him to tell me.

"Well, I had a blow this week. Shawn is supposed to be coming in just under a fortnight, and I've heard from this friend that she can't come after all. It's unlikely now I'll be able to have the boy unless I can find someone else. My daughter can't come. Would you consider coming to help me with him?"

He was looking at me in the most earnest way. I knew how much he was looking forward to his little son's visit. I felt at once flattered and confused.

"How long would it be for?"

"A month. He's due to come on the 28th. I don't want to put you on the spot. You've got your job to think about, I know that. Think it over. There's nearly two weeks to go."

I couldn't pretend that the thought of a whole month over there in those idyllic surroundings didn't appeal strongly. I was already bewitched by the place, the garden, the enchanting creek. Yet I was divided in my loyalty to the company and I was awfully happy with the crazy outfit.

"It does sound tempting" I said, "I'm sure, with you, that I would fall for Shawn. Can I think it over, so much depends on what our producer has to say."

He understood this and he said " Thank you honey."

Autumn Gold

We were outside the corner shop. I waited while he went inside. Afterwards we walked back to the Quay. A whole month with him, I thought, staying in the hut, going out in the boat, swimming in the creek which was like a private pool. The garden with the sloping lawn, the giant sunflowers. And the quiet summer evenings....what bliss. A feeling of delicious happiness stole over me. What an experience it would be....yet I was slightly afraid.

Leo, with his perception, sensed my thoughts.

"You're young and attractive honey, don't I know it, but as I said before, you can trust me, there's no ulterior motive. I just want to be able to give my boy a lovely holiday."

I wondered what the locals would think if they heard that Mr. Walmsley had a girl, an actress, staying with him over at Pont Creek. An eight year old child is no chaperone. I could not help smiling at the thought, the more I did think the more it appealed to me. It would be an adventure, almost a daring thing to do; made more so by the splendid isolation of the hut.

Doreen was still cooling her feet in the water when we got back. She would have been surprised if she had heard us discussing the holiday. Her back view looked all unsuspecting as she sat there. I called out that I'd got some chocolate.

My spirits soared as we got into the boat. The joy of being on the water again! Leo took the oars, and with his approval, I got hold of the line. I would wait until we were clear of the passing traffic of pleasure boats, and those which were moored. Then I would start fishing.

I kept thinking of Leo's proposition. One whole glorious month! I could fish and pull about in the dinghy. I wondered what Doreen would think, and decided to wait a bit before telling her. It was nice to just think about it happily to myself.

Now clear of the boats, I began paying out my line. We were becoming wildly happy and reverting to childish games.

"Knock, knock" Doreen said suddenly. "Who's there?" I answered beginning to chuckle. I'd heard some of her versions before.

"Egbert."

"Egbert who?"

"Egg but no bacon."

Leo didn't exactly fall about laughing but he smiled good naturedly and pulled hard on his left oar to avoid a motorboat coming fast towards us.

"Go on, your turn" Doreen reminded me. In our version of this game we improvised.

"I've got one! I cried.

"A fish? You've got a bite? asked Leo.

"No, an idea. Felix" I said, to Doreen.

"Felix who?"

"Feel excited?" This brought a shriek from her and another smile from Leo. "You'd better keep this for Shawn, he's going to love it."

We grew madder every minute, clowning, pulling faces, making up comic verse. Such juvenile behaviour might have been a reaction to the nervous energy we had expended with so much studying. In spite of this hilarity I remembered the golden rule of sitting still in a boat.

Leo maintained his good humour throughout, and only a shade of vexation crossed his face when Doreen picked up his rucksack and held it over the side of the boat, pretending to drop it. He suggested, nicely, that she might like to take the oars for a bit.

After that we began going madly in all directions which added to the hilarity. Eventually she managed a fairly clear course.

I hooked a fish. It was really exciting. I stood up, as instructed and began hauling the line, hand over hand....and suddenly there it was, squirming to left and right. Seeing its poor startled face I wanted to put it back.

"No you don't my lass!" Leo was indignant. "We're having that for supper; more if we're lucky. Ho! it's a good one, a pollack." Deftly he extracted the hook from its mouth and threw it astern. He re-baited my hook and chucked it overboard leaving me to pay out the line while he baited his own hook. There were two lines as well as a fishing rod. Doreen wanted to try her luck so I finished paying out and changed places with her. She was lucky almost straight away and landed a fine one. Leo had to help her haul it in as it was so heavy. She at once gave a macabre imitation of it with its astonished staring eyes, and opening and shutting mouth.

With fishing you might go on getting one after another. Then your luck changes and they stop biting. Perhaps word gets round that the enemy is riding the water high above them. After Doreen's catch they must have moved away for there were no more bites.

The dinghy was a joy to row, being steady and having momentum. If you stopped rowing she glided on for a bit like a sailing boat. You could get a real speed up if you wanted to. With such weather I was content to go slow. I loved making her glide for then I would lean on the oars and look around and marvel at the beauty of the creek, the high land covered in flowers, the deep blue water.

We were coming to the cove. I brought the boat round until I heard a soft crunch on the shore. The tide was half way up and on the flood, the best time to swim, the water warmed by the shore. "Let's go in" I said to Doreen. We jumped ashore and I fastened the rope to the pulley frape.

"We haven't brought our costumes."

"Yes go in and have a dip" said Leo, "I've got towels."

He was down on one knee gutting the fish with his pen-knife. After a bit more persuasion Doreen agreed and went up for the towels, nearly colliding with Choo-i who was racing down at jet speed to get to the fish. Leo put the gutted fish into a large saucepan taken from the boat. He stood up and looked at the creek. Presently Doreen returned.

"Don't watch us will you? We're going in our underwear."

He laughed, "Get on with you! I'm going up to put the kettle on. I'll call when tea's ready."

When he was out of sight up the path, we stripped off to bra and pants. I splashed straight into the water. It was cold at first but I lied to Doreen, shivering by the edge: "It's warm as toast, come on." Soon I was swimming into patches of really warm water. Doreen shrieked loudly as she went in, as though attacked by maniacs.

There were barnacles, winkles and limpets clinging to the rocks at either side of the cove, and clumps of sea-weed, warm as a blanket to wrap round you. It was thick and elastic with small balloon-like pods, fascinating to pop. In the shallow water we saw several crabs of all sizes and a few microscopic fish. I could have stayed longer but a shout from Leo: "Tea's up" brought us both out. The towels were plain and coarse. We soon got dry and laid our briefs on a big hot step. Leo, leaning on the balcony, smiled at us as we came up the path, cool in our frocks, with soaking hair. Had we enjoyed it? he asked.

"You're going to get a shock when you go in" he told us, "I haven't tidied the place since you were here. We're in a bit of a muddle I'm afraid."

We got a shock alright. Mingled and strewn about the room in glorious confusion were objects so diverse and often so weird that it was like a surrealistic painting; boxes of tin tacks, pairs of socks, a saucepan, fish hooks, a paraffin drum, a large saw, some maps, a heavy rope, pages of manuscript, packets of nails, pencils, paint remover, bitter chocolate, a tin of tar, a ski cap, a landing net and a jar of Marmite. The desk was spilling over with more sheets of manuscript, carbon paper, cigarette ends, lead weights, half empty mugs of coffee, odd pennies, boxes of tobacco, more fish hooks, tea-spoons and stamps. And the typewriter stood heroically among this sea of objects.

Doreen and I gaped at it almost with reverence. Leo; leaning on the door post with a cigarette in hand, watched our reaction with obvious amusement. "It's what you might call lived in" he said. About to sit down, Doreen was startled by a loud shout "HEY!" don't sit there!" Placed lovingly on the settee alongside a pair of hiking boots and some six inch nails, was a line with some large evil-looking fish hooks with feathers attached.

"Charming! Might have done myself a mischief" said Doreen.

"I'll have to get it cleaned up before my boy comes" Leo said ruefully. "Never mind, get your tea while it's hot."

Round the kitchen table we sipped hot tea, sweet and delicious after the swim. I felt so at ease here, so natural as though I had known Leo all my life. Whatever I might decide about the holiday with the little boy, I knew then that I just had to help him now. Here was an early S.O.S. message. Operation clean up.

After tea, Doreen and I went into action. Leo had gone down to the big room for his tobacco. We collected some damp cloths, a broom, a brush and pan and advanced into battle. Snared in his den, he looked up as we came in, sensing danger. Then he noticed the ammunition.

"What on earth?" he began.

"We're going to clean up for you" I told him sweetly. His face registered horror.

"Good God, I don't want you to do that, no no no. Leave it.... It's better to leave the dust to settle. Come on, sit down, I appreciate it very much but...."

But Doreen had already begun with the broom. He was now prowling warily in front of his desk which I was about to wage war on. "Excuse me Leo." I started to collect mugs.

He pounced like a lion.

"No you damn well don't, my lass. By God! Don't touch anything on here. I know just where everything is, my papers, notes about the book." He shuddered at the narrow escape he had had and reached for his tobacco. As he rolled a cigarette he looked fondly at his desk, cigarette ends and all.

After a while he became reconciled and we improvised a mad ballet of the brooms, dancing the dust away, pirouetting with the polish. We managed a near Nureyev leap to get at the cobwebs decorating the ceiling by the door. Leo, now quite diverted, was laughing as he watched from the balcony.

There was another chair he had made himself. Nice and sturdy, very much masculine. Here he liked to sit and relax by the cosy stove which had a line above for socks and handkerchiefs. I was working on that end of the room when I looked up and saw a fascinating cobweb on the ceiling and two spiders. I was wondering what to do with them when Leo put me wise. "Don't disturb Joey and Charlie, they're great friends of mine, I spend hours watching the intricate way they spin their web, absolutely fascinating, a work of art." Thwarted again, I turned my attention to the nice Chinese carpet covering most of the floor. Down on my knees with a stiff brush, I chased away the dust. So many delightful creatures co-habited with Leo that I thought 'he can't possibly be lonely.'

"WATCH IT!" A shout from Doreen. "There's a huge Daddy-Long-Legs creeping up behind you." I sat back on my heels and surveyed it coldly. I had learned to be cautious now. "One of your chums Leo? Or might I persuade it to go outside?"

We worked on, shaking mats, plumping cushions, wet-mopping ledges. We were silent now, feeling the thrill of creation as the room took shape. A smell of lavender filled the air. The windows gleamed bright giving a clear view of the creek. I went and picked some flowers. Leo had gone to dig up some potatoes and pick some runner beans for supper. He wanted us to stay and have the fish.

The room looked lovely when we had finished work. I kept standing back to admire it from all angles. I had just knelt down to pick up the last tin tack from the floor when I saw two sea-boots slowly walking over the carpet on their way to the kitchen. I was about to protest when a voice above them informed me that they had been well and truly rinsed at the stream.

Digging is a strenuous job, as is rowing and pushing boats out. Leo was glad to relax in his chair with the Sunday papers. He was thrilled by the transformation of the room. It would have defeated him, he said. Now he must keep it this way for Shawn's visit.

Doreen and I left him in peace and went to prepare the supper. The fish, all filleted, lay ready on a plate. The potatoes like white marbles, the beans young and juicy looking. We put them all on to cook, first preparing the fish in Leo's way with a dusting of flour, then into hot fat. There was also a crisp lettuce, some watercress and apples. In the garden there were blackcurrant bushes, the fruit ripe and plentiful. We filled a bowl and cooked them with lots of sugar. The meal was nearly ready, the fish nicely brown , and the potatoes now with butter on and smelling of garden mint. We made dressing for the salad and when the fruit was cooked I stirred the cream from the milk into it so it was like a mousse.

The table was set and I went in to call Leo.

He was stretched out in his chair, one foot up on the stove, the fork propped against the wall. I moved closer to him and saw that he was fast asleep, his cheek upon his hand, newspapers across his lap. It was a pose of unconscious charm, the well shaped head, the thick tousled hair, the rust colour of his pullover. It was a shame to wake him. He was all in, tired out. Looking at him I was struck by something in his face, and I think it was then that I came to understand more clearly, what it must be costing him, this exile from the family he loved.

Just then he woke up, saw me and looked startled. "Good God! I passed out completely. What time is it?"

"Supper time, and it does look good." He sat up, looking almost guilty for his nap, and looked round the room. He reached for my hand and gave it a squeeze.

"You are good honey, both of you. Thank you for clearing up, the place looks really exciting now."

"I've just loved it; we've been laughing all the afternoon."

Then I told him. "Leo, please don't worry any more, because if Tony gives permission I will come and help you with your boy."

Again he pressed my hand, and as though for an answer, covered it with his other one. He did not say anything, but I saw his eyes grow misty.

****

It was quite late when Doreen and I started to make our way back to Fowey. The supper had been delicious, a meal straight from the land and sea. It seemed the perfect way to live.

We decided to walk so as to save Leo from having to row back, although he was ready to. At the top of his land were two paths both made by him; one, a spiral which ascended to the top of the valley where it linked with the Polruan path, and a smaller one leading from it down to the pink cottage which lay round the jutting headland. The view from the top of the spiral path was a panorama taking in the whole nine acres of land, the hut, the garden and the creek. It was beautiful, this walk in the hills, with honeysuckle growing wild, filling the air with perfume. The Polruan path followed the creek all along its course to where it widened into the harbour showing a complete view of Fowey by the waterside.

It had not taken us more than twenty minutes to reach Polruan. This was a village-town of great charm, a maze of cobbled streets, alleyways and steep steps leading down to the Quay. Some of the cottages were pastel in colour, and these, together with the houses were built on each side of a steep hill and were divided by the alleyways and cobbled lanes. When we got there the ferry boat was waiting at the Quay.

We spent that night at Esme's cottage where she made us very welcome. The following morning we caught a bus back to Dingle in time for rehearsal. We already knew our lines as this time there were so few to learn.

By now Doreen knew of Leo's proposal that I should help him. Like me she wondered what Tony's reaction would be. If it was favourable I was to phone Esme to give a message to Leo. All the way on the bus I tried to work out how I should broach the subject to Tony.

To my surprise he took it very well. It would have to depend, he said, on whether he could get a replacement for the month, and this would mean advertising. Luckily there was no immediate hurry. Shawn was due to arrive on the 28th of July, the bank holiday weekend. It was only the 16th, twelve days to go. But poor Leo would be keyed up, anxiously waiting for the verdict.

Back in our digs after the show that night, Doreen and I discussed the play **Over The Hill**. Old Mrs. Howard had wrung every heart with her star performance as the floor-scrubbing mother. We could not help chuckling as we recalled some of the melodramatic scenes, and the droll way she gesticulated with her arm thrown out, head thrown back and finger pointing as she uttered the big curtain line at the end of the play: "TO THE WORKHOUSE, OVER THE HILL."

I was in bed, reading another chapter of **Foreigners**. Doreen had read **Love in the Sun** quickly, unable to put it down. I was a slow reader. Often I would turn the book over, to admire again that face on the back cover.

"You like him, don't you" said Doreen. She was brushing her hair at the dressing table, looking at me through the mirror.

Of course I liked him, but more than that, I knew that I had found a very special, unique friend.

" I thought it was so kind of him, that first time we went to The Studio and he told us we could stop with him if ever we were stuck for digs. I love going over there. Without ever being effusive he makes you feel at home."

Still looking at the photo I said "There's much character in his face, don't you think?"

"Yes, and when he told us he was fifty nine I was surprised, for he looks much younger. He's got lots of personality and I think he is very good looking. But he would be more so if he smartened up a bit. Sometimes," she giggled, "he looks a bit funny, especially in that old jacket with the rucksack slung over his back."

But I was remembering how he looked that night he took me to the dance; his hair fresh combed, thick with a wave on top, his bright pullover.

"He is someone you would never forget" I said.

****

CHAPTER IX.

FISH FOR YOUR SUPPER.

I think I was fated to spend that month with Leo and his boy. Everything was going well. The advert was successful and a girl was coming to take my place. Joe would move into the 'nuttery' so Doreen would have company. Leo was overjoyed when he heard the good news. It was arranged that Shawn would be brought down on Saturday, the 29th of July, by a mutual friend of his parents who herself was going on holiday to the Isle of Wight. She would stay overnight and continue her holiday next day.

Our landlady's reaction was interesting. She wouldn't dream of doing such a thing. We were discussing round the table after supper one night.

"Mr. Walmsley lives in a very isolated place" Doreen told her, watching for her reaction, "it's quite inaccessible except by boat, unless you hack your way up the path to the hills."

"And there's no telephone" I added gleefully. "No electric light. He has Tilley lamps, cooks by calor gas and has to do all his shopping by boat."

She looked from one of us to the other as though appealing for reason. As for herself, why she'd be scared to stay with a man she hardly knew, especially if it was as lonely up there as we said. Why, good gracious, she wouldn't think of it!

"Sometimes" I said, piling it on, "the tide goes very far out and there's nothing but mud flats, so if the boat gets stuck then you're really marooned."

"Well! You certainly have some pluck to entertain that idea."

"Would you do it?" I asked Doreen. She hesitated. "I'm not sure really, it's a gorgeous place, but it *is sort of remote isn't it?"*

"But how romantic Doreen."

And Joe, always a cautious one, looked thoughtful. "You might be talked about" he suggested. This hadn't occured to me. For one thing, I was almost unknown by the people of Fowey. I felt a slight twinge of unease, but I just shrugged my shoulders.

"You're not living if you're not talked about Joe."

Then I thought of the friend who had been going to come and look after the little boy. Well certainly she hadn't been bothered about being talked about. I mentioned this to Joe.

"She may look the part" he said "and you don't. You don't fit the governess image, or nanny for that matter."

Fish For Your Supper

"Eight is too old for a nanny."

"That's beside the point. I'm saying you don't look the part. You're an actress, that's what you look like."

"She'll look like nothing on earth when she's stuck in the mud" laughed Doreen, "in old gum boots, pushing and heaving to get the boat afloat."

Joe's remarks did not really bother me. I felt I knew a lot about Leo already. I had only to look again at the back of **Foreigners** and read the tributes from authors like J.B. Priestley, Daphne du Maurier and Lawrence of Arabia. And Daphne herself who was his friend and lived nearby would be sure to say a good word for him.

Until the Bank Holiday I was kept busy with more plays to learn. I looked forward to my new role as housekeeper-cum-nanny, not caring if I looked the part or not. All this time the glorious weather continued, and I set off for Fowey that Sunday morning in a heatwave.

Leo was at the bus stop when I arrived, anxiously looking out for me. He greeted me warmly and said how much he had been looking forward to the holiday. When we reached the Quay I noticed his boat had been smartened up with fresh touches of scarlet and blue paint.

"Why she does look smart" I said. "Can I pull?" I had such a longing to take the oars once again, to feel them beneath my grasp. There wasn't a breath of wind. Leo was happy for me to take over. He was full of his boy.

"All's going well" he said "I've been on tenter-hooks in case he wouldn't be allowed to come at the last minute, or that he might turn round and say that he wants to go home. But he's been lovely, gave me a smile when I met him and asked about Choo-i. He's very interested in you by the way, I've told him all about you."

The dinghy was a grand boat to pull. Even though the oars were rather heavy and the boat a large one, I could manage to make her go at really good speed. As we came in sight of the cove it all looked dear and familiar, the steps, the path leading up to the hut.

Leo shouted "HOY!"

Slowly I pulled in until I heard the boat go crunch as she grounded on the foreshore. As we got out a voice called back "Hello" and looking up I saw a woman coming down the path with a little boy dressed only in shorts. He started to run until he reached the boat where he proceeded with expertise to moor her on the pulley rope. Presently the woman joined us. She was introduced to me as Pam. At a rough guess she could have been about thirty -five and she loked thoroughly capable of having charge of a child.

"Come on my lad" said Leo "Meet this very nice girl I've been telling you about." The small boy gave another pull on the rope and came over to me.

"Shake hands with her" laughed Leo "They teach you all that in your swank public school don't they?" A small brown hand was offered and the child looked up at me with a little self-conscious smile. I saw then that he was beautiful. His eyes were large and dark; compelling. Like some lovely gypsy child his complexion was rose-tan, his body tanned all over. I pictured him with earrings and a red spotted scarf round his head.

We all walked up the path. A red tartan rug was laid out on the lawn with a book on it, open, face down. On the grass a beach towel was stretched out to dry. Leo introduced us.

"Plenty of room on the rug" said Pam. She had a nice fresh complexion and short brown hair. Shawn had been in the water just before we came, she told Leo. He had swum very well. He had wanted to stay in longer but she had to be firm when it was time to come in.

"You would still be in now if you had your way, wouldn't you?" she said and rubbed his head affectionately. Then she went indoors to prepare lunch, refusing offers of help.

Shawn, still a bit shy of me, followed after her.

"What do you think of him?" asked Leo.

"I never imagined him like this. He's like a Greek God."

I could detect parental pride when Leo said, "He's a good lad. Those front teeth need straightening a bit though."

Before lunch Pam suggested that Shawn might like to wash his hands. I sensed he didn't, but was on his best behaviour.

The young Greek God had a hearty appetite, especially for Pam's apple pie. He went on sweetening it lavishly until his father rebuked him.

"We might go fishing later on when we take Pam across" said Leo. The boy's eyes sparkled.

"Can we go out to sea?"

"It's a long way Shawn, and who's going to do all the rowing?"

"I will!" He was on to his second helping of pie now. "I'll pull all the way there and back." Leo smiled.

"Go on with you. No, we'll go up river to the jetties and drop Pam ashore by the station for her train."

The tide had ebbed considerably since we arrived and was still doing so. To keep afloat the dinghy had to be put on a trip anchor. I went down

78

with Leo and Shawn to watch this operation which was useful to learn. Shawn rowed us towards the bluff of the cove and we disembarked on some rocks. There were two painters. One was attached to a ring at the bow of the boat , the other was unattached, longer and tarred. Leo tied the shorter rope through the ring of a flat anchor which he had laid on the right side of the dinghy. It was important to get the balance right so that it lay half on and half off the edge. Next he tied the end of the black rope on to the other one and gave the boat a firm push, not too hard in case it disturbed the anchor too soon. The boat then glided away. When she reached her full span he gave a sharp jerk with the black rope and the anchor fell into the water. It required skill to do this as sometimes the anchor would fall overboard while the boat was still gliding. This procedure kept the boat afloat for a reasonable time during an ebb tide but on a low Spring tide the creek became completely dry , exposing the mud flats. If it was necessary to keep the boat afloat for a long time she would have to be rowed past the bluff to a sandy bay called Brazen Island which lay near the Polruan shipyard; here she would be moored by the shorter rope to the anchor which would be taken ashore. By this time the tide would have ebbed so far that it would be possible to walk back along the foreshore.

After we had finished mooring I felt that I had learned quite a lot about handling a boat. We walked back up the path and my heart felt light. I was in for an adventure.

Some hours later the men came back with four pollack. Shawn was excited, his eyes shining. He held up a big fat fish for me to see.

"Look! I got the biggest. Look at this one ! It pulled and tugged on the line, didn't it Daddy?"

"Yes, it's a beauty. You caught most of them didn't you?"

"Can we have them for supper? I want to eat this one." Leo carried the bucket over to the sink.

"Come and watch me fillet them first and you'll learn something."

They were happy after the trip. Shawn insisted on cooking his own fish.

It was nearly dusk. Time to light the Tilley lamps. There was one in the big room and one in the kitchen. Leo lit both, then he assembled the three Aladdin lamps and refilled them with paraffin. The Tilley lamp made a slight hissing noise. It shone brightly down on us at the supper table. We had some fried potatoes with the fish, bread and butter and tea. I had the feeling of having stepped right back in time. Apart from the odd motorboat chugging by, it might have been the year 1860, with no electricity or telephone and water pumped from the stream.

Shortly after supper Shawn was packed off unwillingly to bed.

Our first evening alone together. Leo in his chair with an eye-shade on and both feet up on the stove. Me in an easy chair next to him. He rolled me a cigarette and one for himself. Then he breathed a sigh of contentment, and possibly relief.

"Thank God it's worked out so well. I wish you could have seen his face when he was hauling in that fish. He won't forget that. He is a lovely boy."

We sat there for some time. So quiet it was. A rowing boat went gliding up the creek. Gentle sounds of rowlocks squeaking and the oars dipping into the water. I stretched my arms.

"Tired?" asked Leo, catching hold of my hand.

"Only a bit."

"Let's take a walk down to the cove."

The tide had come right up. The water, now inky dark, was lapping against the first step. The air had gone cool, drenched with the scent of honeysuckle. A sudden rustling noise came from the water. "Hear that?" said Leo "that was a cormorant. They dive right down for their prey, gobble up a fish and bob up again. Underwater hunters, blast them. But it shows the fish are about."

Going back up the path he asked me casually, would I like this kind of life? Was I keen on gardening, growing flowers? At that moment we passed the giant sunflowers. We noticed that Shawn's lamp was still on so we went in through the back door to his room. He was fast asleep. A book lay open beside him. Leo, looking to see if it was one of his, said, "He's dreaming of that big fish he caught," and turned out the lamp above the child's head.

My bedroom was next to the kitchen on the right, Shawn's was opposite.

"I hope you're not an early riser" Leo said, putting the kettle on, "because I can't see things moving in front of my eyes first thing, not until I've had my tea and toast and thought things out. I'll give you a shout when I've finished. Will one bottle be enough?" He was unscrewing the top of a hot water bottle.

"I doubt if I want one" I said, surprised. It was a warm summer night.

"I couldn't sleep without two. Got no fat on me and I feel the cold a lot."

When he first told me that I could trust him as he had no ulterior motive in wanting me to stay for the month, he made a joke of it, saying he would keep at arms length. Now as he wished me good night he deliberately stepped back the length of two arms.

"Keeping my promise aren't I?"

I carried my Aladdin lamp to my room and felt like Jane Eyre going to bed. I made up the bed with thick flannelette sheets and khaki and grey coloured blankets. The sheets were slightly coarse but warm and nice. Through the thin partition dividing my room from the kitchen I could hear Leo moving about in his stockinged feet filling his hot water bottles. Sometimes I fancied I heard him talk softly to himself. I wondered what my landlady would think now if she were in my shoes, or rather my bed.

I blew out the lamp and settled down to sleep. The freshwater stream gurgled as it ran down to the cove. I lay there absorbing the newness of my surroundings, the different noises. The kettle being moved from the gas stove, the water spluttering, choking into the bottle. Soft footsteps, then the kitchen door closing. A cow bellowed from the nearest farm, and somewhere, far in the distance, a night owl hooted.

A treble voice, sweet and true, came through my dreams. Under the weight of sleep I could discern the bawdy words of a sea shanty. "Once aboard the lugger an' the girl is mine, the girl is mine." Pattering footsteps, the clink of china, a cupboard door opening. Through the thin partition even the slightest noise could be heard. The merry voiced boy didn't know he was breaking rules. The kitchen door opened, and a now familiar voice, sounding put out,

"What are you doing Shawn? Go back to bed until I've had my breakfast, then you can get yours."

"Oh Daddy!"

"Yes come on now. I must have peace first thing."

"But I want mine. I won't make a noise."

"You'll get it later, go on, there's a good lad."

"Oh gosh, honestly!" Disgruntled mutterings and he was bundled out.

Soon a delicious smell of toast came wafting through to the 'prisoners' in their rooms. Then a friendly sound of tea being poured. I called out a greeting to Shawn. He came into my room already dressed in jeans and a tee shirt.

"Daddy won't let me be in the kitchen" he said, his lovely face dark with resentment, "and I'm hungry and it's jolly unfair."

"He won't be long. That's a nice outfit you're wearing." This diverted him from his woes for a while.

"Seen my badge?" He proudly displayed the one on his shirt with the letters R.S.P.C.A. "I've been a member for a year." We chatted for a bit, but sounds from the kitchen distracted him. More hopeful sounds now like a chair being scraped back, a match being struck. Then the much awaited,"All clear!"

Shawn, like a sprinter, almost dived through the door into the kitchen. Leo called to me. "Did you sleep well honey? There's some toast here for you."

As I was getting dressed I overheard a curious conversation.

"I do wish Amanda was here."

"Well, with any luck I might be able to fetch her this morning."

"Where is she?"

"Over at Polruan. She's given me a lot of worry the last few weeks."

"What's wrong with her?"

"Nothing very much, playing me up mostly. I'm not standing any more nonsense from her." Was this one of his children, I wondered. A girl friend?

"Daddy, can I go with you to fetch her? Shall we take her with us if we go to sea?"

"That depends if she behaves herself. You can come with me if you're quick. I'm going down to the boat now. I'll be about five minutes."

To me he called "We're going to Polruan. We won't be long." I went into the kitchen where Shawn was hurriedly tying his shoe laces. I was just about to ask, "Who is Amanda?" when he said, "We're going to Polruan," and rushed out, shouting "Wait for me Daddy!"

The first glimpse I had of my rival was from the front room. I was giving it a surface tidying, careful to avoid the desk and the two pet spiders. A noise brought me to the window, the loud chugging of an engine. I could see a small motorboat with the dinghy in tow. Shawn was at the steering wheel, his father astern,one hand on the tiller (just in case). As I walked down the path to get a better view, the engine slowed down until the boat was within a few feet of the buoy. Leo, with astonishing agility, leant over the side, grabbed the buoy, and then, still holding it, climbed up onto the deck and began fixing it to the chain. The boat had what appeared to be a very small cabin and a tall mast with a flag on the top. Shawn saw me and shouted, "Did you see me steering? I steered all the way." Leo shouted, "Untie the painter and bring the dinghy round." The boy did so and brought the boat alongside the other one. Leo held on while Shawn got in first and grabbed the oars, and they pulled in.

That afternoon I set out for my first trip in *Amanda*. She had been over in the shipyard having her engine checked. Leo hoped she would be in fettle. We were not taking the dinghy, but there was a pair of oars in the boat as a precaution. It was sunny and slightly breezy. We took the two fishing lines and the rod. As soon as we went aboard Shawn busied himself with his special jobs. He took the engine cover off and pumped the water out. Leo, about to start the engine, folded his hands and uttered a mock prayer. "Now my darling, are you going to to start first time or are you going to play me up?" Shawn turned on the petrol. Leo swung the engine. Not a sound. He tried again. Still nothing. The third time she tuned up quite hopefully, then, after a few seconds, petered out. He took off the engine cover, cleaned the plugs and tried again. This brought no response. He looked exasperated and scratched his head.

"Oh hell, damn it" he said softly.

"Daddy!"

"Pass me a spanner please" said Leo distracted. Shawn got it for him. It took about fifteen minutes before the temperamental *Amanda* would come out of her sulk. Then after about eight turns we heard the chug, chug ...... Leo closed the throttle down, quickly went forward to cast off, but as he was about to do so, she stopped dead.

"You bitch!" said Leo not so softly.

Shawn was getting disgruntled, "Oh why won't she start?" he kept saying. "I thought we were going to have a nice trip." Leo was calm and patient with him, sometimes asking for certain tools or a rag.

Just as we were about to call it a day, the engine made a roaring, spluttering sound and miraculously maintained her chugging noise. Leo shouted "Hooray!" and kept her just ticking over. Then he leapt like a mountain goat on to the fore-deck and cast off.

I sat beside Leo at the stern, Shawn was at the helm, sitting on the top deck. He was happy now, one hand on the mast, screwing up his eyes against the bright sun. The wind was blowing my hair madly about. "Can we go faster?" shouted Shawn. Leo shook his head. He had to go easy on petrol. While he prepared the lines and baited the hooks, I took the tiller. It gave me a lovely new feeling of responsibility and temporary ownership. At close quarters I could observe *Amanda*. There was a small seat just near the steering wheel on her port side, and opposite to starboard, an even smaller one. The cabin was small but with just enough room to shelter two people comfortably. There was a little shelf at the far end where the tools were kept. Under both seats were two oil drums for ballast, and a narrow seat ran along her port side. A waterproof cover, made by Leo, fitted over the engine lid, and there were various tools, bits of rope, a funnel, compass anchor and cans of petrol.

As soon as we approached the harbour, Leo suggested taking over. With all the yachts and cruisers it could be tricky weaving between the different craft. But I was power drunk by now and didn't want to relinquish my hold on the tiller. I wasn't doing too badly. If I became dreamy and my gaze wandered out to sea, Shawn, who had been made to get down from the deck would shout, "Look out!" and Leo would grasp the tiller and give a dramatic swerve to left or right.

Leo had baited two trolling lines, and having changed places with Shawn, gave one to him, the other to me, which he had payed out as I was steering. He instructed Shawn about the amount of line to use. We were past the harbour now and within sight of Readymoney Cove. I was to keep close to the Fowey side. Because of *Amanda's* recent behaviour we wouldn't go too far out to sea, although both wind and tide would be favourable coming back.

I looped my line round my wrist so as to leave me free to steer. I was first to land a fish, a good sized pollack. Leo took the wheel as I hauled it in. Shawn immediately announced that he had a bite too. He was right, only there wasn't a fish on his line, it had just taken the bait. Shortly after this I hooked another. Shawn now saw me as a rival. Goaded and mad to catch one, he rebaited his hook and kept pulling his line to feel for a fish. It was too much for him when I caught another one.

"Why haven't I got one yet? She's got three." He was cross with his father and cross with me.

We had passed Coombe Cove, the next, but not so popular as Readymoney, and we were not far off Pridmouth Bay, Leo's favourite when, for no apparent reason *Amanda's* engine stopped. It could have been alarming if the wind had been in the other direction, but as it was we merely drifted back to Readymoney Cove.

Shawn was feeling very unhappy. "First I don't get any fish, then the engine goes wrong, it's jolly mean."

"And who caught them last night?"

Amanda wouldn't budge. Leo tried everything. We carried on fishing until the wind took us back to harbour, where we had to haul in the lines.

Leo had begun to row. I took over from him when we got to the mouth of Pont Creek. It was a strange feeling to be pulling a motorboat. We didn't seem to be getting anywhere. *Amanda* should go on a diet, I thought. It was really a sweat getting her to move. Then Leo took the other oar and we made slow, but steady progress. Shawn, arms folded and still very cross, sat in the stern.

Eventually, 'years' later, as we were coming into the cove, Leo said to his boy "I think I know why *Amanda* conked out on us." Shawn pretended that he wasn't interested in knowing. Then, presently;

"Well?"

"She's jealous?"

"Jealous?"

"Yes, can't you guess?" He thought for a moment and then smiled in spite of himself.

"Stephanie!"

"You've hit it."

Leo settled her for the night, covering her engine and tying her to the buoy. Then we climbed aboard the dinghy and as we made for the shore I looked back at *Amanda*, secure on her moorings. She had three portholes on each side. They were like large reproachful eyes. I fancied she was looking at me, weighing me up.

"Good night my darling" Leo called out to her. "Bitch! Butter wouldn't melt in your mouth to look at you now."

Apart from my love of the country and of the sea, of the pleasure I got from cycling, swimming and rowing boats, I was not the sporty type. Once, as a child, I had caught some mackerel while on holiday in Devon with my family. That had been fun, so had the holiday. But I had never hankered to repeat the fishing trip. To me, sport was a number one bore, along with the people who talked about it.

What then, was I doing in gum boots hauling in fish? All my interests at that time were centred on the stage and screen, dancing and music. With anyone else I would have been very bored, but Leo made it interesting. He had a strong, magnetic personality, it was being with him that mattered. A country walk became an adventure. He knew the name of every tree and hedge-side flower.

During the holiday I got to know him well. There were so many aspects of him. The author with his pipe, sitting in his chair, one foot up on the stove, eyes bright with reminiscing, warm, relaxed. The ardent fisherman with his love of the sea and boats. *Amanda*, 'the other woman'. The gardener, growing his perfect potatoes, scarlet runners, spinach and kale. The naturalist, knowing the name of every plant, the habits of every bird and fish. The teacher showing his boy how to use a rod and showing me how to haul in a catch, tie reef knots and moor the boat. His affection for the boy, shown in many ways, like the joy in seeing him catch a fish and making him a plaster cast.

The days were filled with interest, there was always something to do, some planned excursion. As well as fishing and boating, there were picnics at the various coves and beaches, country walks that led to the sea, tramping across fields and clambering down rocks. River trips, calling on friends, going to the club. Bathing in the creek and catching fat prawns at the flood tide.

The evenings had a special charm, with just the two of us together. If it turned chilly we lit the cosy stove. Sometimes when the wind sprang up the Tilley lamp would gently sway as though it were on a ship. And if it chanced to rain, how snug we felt inside as it pattered on the corrugated roof.

It was here that I heard about Leo's early life, of a childhood spent at Robin Hood's Bay on the Yorkshire coast, and his affection for the village. I learnt how he hated school, played truant to go fishing and bird nesting, and had his ears boxed for not knowing his sums. He told me of his early interest in marine biology and natural history and how he started writing articles for magazines when he was a teenager.

I listened enthralled while he recounted his terrifying experiences during World War One when he had joined up as an observer in the Royal Flying Corps. He was sent out to East Africa and was the first to fly over Lake Nyassa. I wondered how he survived fourteen air crashes, being nearly burnt alive in the last one. All this was recalled without a trace of boasting. Then I got him to describe how he won the Military Cross, and this is what he told me.

On one occasion when he and the pilot were flying together, the petrol pipe was severed by an anti-aircraft shell. There was an immediate danger of the engine catching fire and both men being burnt to death. The pilot stayed in the cock-pit and tried to keep the plane on an even keel. Leo climbed out on to the open wing of the aeroplane, crouched down and held the petrol pipe together with his two hands. He managed somehow to wrap his scarf around the pipe which was burning hot, this prevented his hands from being severely burnt. To get to the pipe he had to pass the pilot's cock-pit and to crawl onto the wing. With all his strength he went on holding the pipe, forcing the broken ends together. He kept this up until the pilot was able to make a safe landing.

It had been a proud day for Leo when he went to Buckingham Palace to receive his decoration and heard King George the fifth say as he pinned on the medal: "Very pleased to give you the Military Cross."

It seemed that Leo had never been afraid to take on a challenge, and for a writer he had a strong practical side. My mind would reel when he threw off a careless remark like, "That was when I farmed forty acres of rough land after we took this mansion in Wales. My God, it was exciting when we built the dam." How does one set about building a dam or for that matter, installing a waterwheel and get it going, or build a home out of an old stone barn on the Yorkshire Moors?

Giving the fire a poke he would stagger me by saying, "I'll never forget the children's faces when they first saw the trap I'd built for the pony."

He talked a lot about his children and was always hoping for letters from them. Ann, his eldest, was twenty. She was the baby 'Amelia' in **Love in the Sun** and as stage-struck as me. He was glad he had managed to put her to R.A.D.A. Once he went along and watched her having a fencing lesson. From photographs I could see that Ann was very attractive, slim and graceful, and Henrietta, two years younger, was the outdoor type, sturdy and jolly with a pretty face and fair complexion. She was hoping to go to Alberta, Canada and stay with her father's friends who had a ranch. Simon, his third child was also fair and tall. I was told he had a gentle, quiet personality and had been to Pangborn, without Leo's blessing for he thought him unsuitable for it. It was sad to see photos of Dain Patrick who had been tragically killed in an accident. According to his brothers and sisters he had been "the nicest of us all." He was small and dark with a lot of vitality and resembled his father in looks more than the others.

****

CHAPTER X.

FUN AND NICENESS.

One warm day we set off to walk some four miles to Lantivet Bay. This could be reached by boat, but you could not be sure of the weather conditions for it lay to the east of the harbour mouth. A treacherous wind could spring up suddenly and if the engine failed we would be in a fix.

We might have been on an expedition. Leo insisted in carrying nearly everything in his rucksack slung across his back. Into that went towels, sweaters, swimsuits, fishing tackle and a bottle of milk. He even carried the old black kettle by looping it over a big stick and bearing it on his shoulder. It was half filled with water, enough for our needs. I carried the food and the fishing rods, while we left Shawn to carry a bag of plums, his passion, which curiously got lighter with each step.

There were puffs of white cloud in the very blue sky and a welcome breeze to keep us cool. We went up the spiral path from the garden, on to the main one and crossed the fields which led to Atlantic Road. It was a long climb. Shawn and I were tired when we reached the top. We paused for breath.

"Come on" Leo called, not waiting, "We've a way to go yet."

The road led to Looe about eight miles away. There were fields on each side, those on the right sweeping down to the sea. The view was heavenly. Leo had to stop to admire it. The road dipped down at one point, then rose and after about a mile we turned right and went along a lane running between the fields towards the sea. At the end of the lane we crossed a stile into a sloping field. By now I was feeling hot and the water below looked tempting. Like Shawn I wore shorts and a light top, while Leo was in denim trousers and open neck shirt.

"Are we nearly there?" asked Shawn, suddenly flopping on to the grass. "I want to stay here for a bit. Can I have a drink?" I sat down and fished out some lemonade from my basket.

"Don't mess about Shawn" said his father "We want to get there, come on drink up."

When we got to the end of the field we carried on bearing left, over a stile, through to another that sloped more steeply down and ended at the cliff. To get to the bay we had to climb right down. It wasn't exactly vertical but it took some thinking out and careful foot work. Leo was sure footed and knew where to tread. To help me until I got used to it, he made foot holds with his cupped hands for me to tread on.

We had come to an enchanting spot with several coves to explore, rocks to climb and quite a large cave which Shawn ran into straight away. Leo put our food and the bottle of milk in the cave to keep it cool for it was now very hot. The beach here was similar to White House Beach. There were little pools among the rocks but the those here were bigger and warmer.

"We'll go to the island first" Leo said "and put the rest of our stuff there and have tea later. Are you going to fish now Shawn?"

The island was actually the grassy top of a very big rock that jutted out and became an island when the tide came in. I settled down happily on it, spread out our things and thought of the swim I was going to have in one of the pools.

Leo and Shawn, each with a rod, went off to fish from the rocks. I put on my swim suit. It was not an ideal place for swimming as there were so many rocks and the water gushed and sucked up to them with great force. It almost pushed you back on to them before sucking away again. In some places, where a shadow was cast, the water was a dark, wicked blue, in others a light turquoise. I went in from one of the rocks and was immediately out of my depth. I swam out a bit, clear of them and called out to the fishermen. Leo shouted to be careful. I was having a lovely time and finished off in one of the pools, sitting safe and warm in the deep water.

They caught three wrasse between them, and after Shawn had his swim we set about collecting big stones to make a place to build a fire and boil the kettle. We gathered clumps of dried grass and sticks from the ragged ledges of the cliff, and hunted for twigs.

Leo arranged the stones, the grass and sticks, and soon had a good fire going. The black kettle was soon singing.

"We're having a day of fun and niceness aren't we?" said Shawn.

He was crouching down watching the kettle, ready to tell us when it had boiled. Watching with him, I knew I would never forget this day, and in the years to come, my mind would hold a picture of it.

Leo heaped spoonfuls of tea into the boiling kettle and carried it up to the island. We laid the food out, tomato and watercress sandwiches, chocolate biscuits and the good old jam roll.

How quiet it was, not a single person in sight. Far out on the horizon a ship went slowly by. I felt so good after the long walk and the swim. The sun was beating down drying my wet hair, warming me through like the hot tea. I poured myself out some more. We were using small twigs to stir our tea. Why bother with spoons?

Leo was looking at the ship through his binoculars. "I 'spect that's a cargo ship." said Shawn "Can I have a turn next? Do you think she's coming into Fowey for china clay?" He didn't want to miss anything. It was his vitality and alertness that made him so engaging. He now had an even deeper tan than when he first arrived and it gave him a real swarthy look.

Gloriously tired, I stretched out on the soft grass. Shawn copied me, making a pillow of his sweater. He lay on his bed of green looking up at the sky.

"Let's stay the night here! All night on the island!"

Something of the child in me stirred....it was so perfect here. H   e rolled over to face me. "Shall we? It would be such fun. We could have a midnight swim and after make a fresh fire to warm us."

"And cook the wrasse for our supper." (Shame on you Miss Gubbins, you're playing the role of nanny, remember?)

"We'd see the dawn rise. Wouldn't that be lovely? Then later we'd get up an' catch more fish for breakfast."

I was pondering, drowsily, on how we would keep warm at night when the practical voice of Leo cut in.

"Don't be daft. What would you do when it turned cold?"

"Run about. And put my sweater on." He had an answer for everything. Leo wouldn't be drawn.

Luckily Shawn didn't persist, and like a butterfly, soon settled for something else and went away to explore and climb.

I don't know how long we stayed on the island, only that I was loathe to leave it. Leo sat smoking, looking out at the view. He fished from his pocket a small artist's pad, and with a few deft strokes began to sketch.

"I'm going to hate it when he's gone" he said suddenly. I felt for him then.

"And I'm going to miss you too Stevey. You don't know what it's meant to me having you here."

I sat up and moved closer to him. Suddenly I felt shy. Although natural with him I was inhibited about showing my true feelings. Always they seemed locked inside me. I wanted to say, I love being with you, you make everything real, you've shown me a way of life different from anything I've ever known.

He went on sketching the view, lightly, loving what he saw. I watched for a while, then he surprised me by saying; "You're rather lovely, how is it you're not married?" I hesitated. The question evoked a latent feeling of inadequacy. Perhaps every unmarried girl feels this at being asked such a leading question.

To cover my embarrassment I smiled and said, "I nearly was once, no twice to be exact." I then went on to tell him about my various suitors.

"It often happened that I would have several boy friends around to go out with or else none at all. On one occasion two boys arrived at the same time to take me out. So embarrassing! I couldn't face the situation so I got my mother to answer the door while I hid in my room, chewing my nails."

Leo laughed.

"You could make a comedy out of that. Were they annoyed?"

"Quite a bit. It must have looked as though I was playing them off. But really I wasn't. And they were both so attractive.... I just got awfully vague about things like dates."

He drew me on to hear more, fascinated, seeing it all as a play.

It was getting late. Time to pack up, for we had a long climb ahead. I went to tell Shawn. He was peering into a pool that had two little crabs in it. He protested against going and quickly resumed his rock climbing, leaping in a frenzy from one to another. I turned to go back to the island for our gear when a shout from Shawn made me turn round. He had scrambled down and was running the opposite way and shouting, "Daphne! Daphne!"

Hesitant at first, I followed him until I approached a tall slim beautiful woman. She was wearing elegantly cut white trousers and a tunic top. Her hair was soft yellow and she wore a nautical cap with a peak. Her eyes were bright blue and she was lightly made up. She looked as though she might have stepped out of the pages of Vogue magazine. As the little boy rushed up to her she smiled. Beside her stood a tall handsome man and two demure, pretty young girls.

Hearing the voices brought Leo over and I was introduced to Daphne du Maurier, her husband General Sir Frederick Browning and their two daughters Tessa and Flavia. The girls smiled shyly at me. Daphne and Leo chatted together and she asked him about his other children. The General made polite conversation with me and asked if I was on holiday. They had come round in their boat with George, one of the locals from Polruan who looked after their craft. He had stayed on board.

"Let me see, how old is he now Leo?" Daphne asked, looking at Shawn.

"I'm nearly eight and a half" he piped, smiling up at her. He was thrilled to see her again.

"Do you remember me taking you to see Daphne a couple of years ago?" said Leo. "We went to have tea with her and you rode on my shoulders part of the way home. You're not going to do that today my boy." There was general laughter, some more talk and then we went our separate ways.

It was a steep climb going back. Up the cliff, up through the two fields. Even Leo had to stop to rest before we got to the second one. When at last we were on the road he began telling me about his long friendship with Daphne and her husband. He had known her before she was married. The couple had sailed in their boat to their wedding in the lovely old church at Lanteglos. In Leo's **Love in the Sun** days, she would often row up the creek to see him and 'Dain' and have tea with them. They joined up for picnics and swam together. It was Tommy, Daphne's husband, who rushed 'Dain' to the maternity home at Looe when one of her babies started to arrive early. He brought some of Tessa's baby clothes with him for the new baby.

****

CHAPTER XI.

THE BOY FRIEND.

During my stay at Pont Creek I had enrolled as a temporary member of The Gallants' Sailing Club. It was a friendly place to pop into. Leo was a full time member and sometimes Shawn would go along with me and we played ping pong (a game Leo scorned) or darts. It was here that I met a young undergraduate from Cambridge. He was spending the holidays working in one of the local hotels. His name was Colin and he was tall, nice looking, and obviously on the look out for a girl friend. Most of the times that I went to the club he was there, usually sitting in one of the armchairs, flicking over the pages of a magazine. He would look up when he saw me come in as though half expecting me. He had a cheery face and a wide grin.

I was there one afternoon, playing records and waiting for Leo and Shawn to collect me. They had gone fishing but as it was a damp day I did not feel drawn to going out to sea. As usual Colin was there and he told me about a dance at the club that night.If I would like to go he would call for me perhaps. Obviously he was unaware of the geography of Pont Creek! I liked dancing, but I felt I should confer with Leo first for he might have planned something else. We were discussing it when Leo and Shawn returned. I introduced them. Colin was thrilled to meet an author for the first time. He had just read *Love in the Sun* and had enjoyed it very much. Was Mr Walmsley living in the very place described in the book? As for himself, he too had done a bit of scribbling.... he would be glad of an opinion on it.

Leo, though pleased by the young man's remarks, looked wary. He said he would always try to help anyone trying to write. As for the dance he said it would be nice for me to have an evening out. He hoped however, that it wouldn't go on too late as he got bothered about the tides.

Going back in the boat Leo was quiet and preoccupied. He must have been sending out electric messages all over the place for I could sense that he did not want me to go to this dance. Maybe I was imagining it, for he knew I liked dancing. It was true we had grown closer lately, and breaking the 'arms length' agreement, he sometimes put an arm around my shoulders when he thanked me for a meal I had cooked. Apart from that and the goodnight kiss he gave me on the cheek, we were just friends. Besides, he had told me from the first that he was still in love with his wife.

I banished these thoughts from my mind and after supper began to get ready for my night out.

I put on a pretty dress, fluffed out my hair in a becoming way, then a touch of make-up, a touch of perfume and I stood up and surveyed myself in the mirror.

When Leo saw me he raised his eyebrows in surprise.

When Shawn saw me he said "Gosh! You look .....different."

It was the first time I had dolled myself up during the holiday, and worn something other than a blouse and skirt, shorts or jeans.

"I won't say I don't feel a bit jealous" Leo said as he went down to the water to see me off, "but I hope you have a good time. If you moor the boat to the club railings she should stay afloat for about four hours." Then with a look of appraisal, and something deeper, wistful perhaps, he added,

"You look lovely. If only I had the brass I'd like to take you out to dinner."

I went off with a light heart to row myself to the dance. The water was calm and still, the only ripple caused by the dipping of the oars.

At the end of the creek I turned up-river making for the club. I could already hear the sound of music coming across the river.

Colin was waiting outside the club on the landing stage. He was wearing a dark jacket over light grey trousers with a cream shirt and blue striped tie.

"It's packed out in there" he told me as I approached the steps, "throw up the rope and I'll tie her up."

We hadn't been inside the club for more than a few minutes when a jovial looking man came over.

"Glad you managed to come to our little hop" he said. I recognised him as Wilfred, the club secretary and founder.

Colin had begun jigging to the music, fingers snapping, feet tapping.

"Like a drink or a dance first?" he asked.

"Let's dance."

He was a lively person on the floor, bobbing about and whirling me around.

"Rock, rock, rock around the clock" the vocalist's voice came out loud from the record player and the dancers obeyed. A lock of hair fell over Colin's face. He loosened his tie. Someone trod on my toe.

"OUCH!"

"Oh I say, frightfully sorry!"

"Alright" said Colin, dancing with total abandon, flinging himself all over the place, now moving forward, now back.

"I'm OK" I said, wincing. It was hot work this dance and the floor was crowded.

Next it was 'The Gay Gordons'. We lined up in pairs. Then round and round the room we went. A plump jolly girl called out that she was staying at the pink cottage near me.

"Oh I know, round the bend!" I shouted, not meaning to quip, and then I lost sight of her in this marching, skipping, twirling dance that seemed to have no end.

When the music finally stopped we began weaving our way to the bar. Only soft drinks and snacks were served. We found two vacant chairs and sat sipping coke.

"I am glad you were able to come" Colin said, edging closer and blinking slightly "How much longer are you staying over at the creek?"

"I've another week."

Wilfred called out "Take your partners for the 'Paul Jones'." We stayed put, watching the two circles of hopeful people walking their opposite ways, men hunting girls, girls hunting men. The losers slunk off back to their seats or the bar.

"On my day off" Colin said, "I'd like to come and see you acting."

"You'd better not! You might be disillusioned."

A waltz struck up. Colin took my drink, "Come on."

As we danced he held me close. " I had a feeling I was going to meet a girl like you" he said, drawing me tighter towards him.

I felt slightly uneasy. I liked him, he was fun with his high spirits, his enthusiasm for rock. But I was remembering the look on Leo's face when I introduced him. Suddenly life was becoming complicated.

After the waltz we went on to the balcony. It was then that I heard a tune that was forever to haunt me and remind me of Fowey and that summer night at the club. It came floating through the french windows. I looked out on the dark water, listening.

"I love this tune" said Colin. "It's from the film 'Limelight'. It really does things to me."

The music, so poignant, rose and swelled out as though coming from everywhere, the river, the banks. It tugged at me.

"What are you thinking?"

"It's beautiful, that's what I'm thinking, and a little bit sad like autumn leaves falling; it seems to have the very feel of this place, the lights on the river, the boats and the hut where I'm staying at the creek..." I broke off, remembering how soon I would be leaving it all, and my eyes pricked with sudden tears.

"Shall I see you tomorrow?"

This was unexpected and took me by surprise. I didn't feel quite free to make plans so I hesitated.

"I thought a walk would be nice... the Hall Walk; I'd like to take you there."

"I should love it, but you can see it's just a bit awkward. I've got a job helping out with this little boy."

"Oh I see, but you're free in the evenings aren't you? You must come to the big Regatta do on Saturday. Everyone's going in fancy dress and they're hiring a band."

"You can count on me for that. I just love dressing up."

The dance was nearly over. People were going for their coats. Some would be walking home, others going by car. Not many, I thought, would be using my form of transport. I felt a thrill of pride as we went along towards the boat. I looked lovingly at her as Colin untied the painter. She was waiting for me like a friend, loyal, sturdy in her dark coat of paint. Good girl to wait for me, I thought. I almost patted her.

"Are you alright?" said Colin, after I had stepped in. He gave the boat a push and I took the oars. "Can you see your way properly....don't forget the fancy dress party.... it starts at eight." His voice trailed off. I could see quite well across the harbour because of the lights shining on the water. A midnight row. What bliss. After I had gone a few yards I stopped rowing, happy to be just still. It was strange to reflect that only a few weeks ago Cornwall had been only a name to me. A motorboat went past, heading down river. A chorus of men's voices rang out, rich and tuneful: 'Michael row the boat ashore, hallelujah! Michael row the boat ashore....'

It was really exciting to be out on the water at night. I started rowing again. I was crossing the harbour now and as I turned up the creek I noticed how dark it was. But I was not bothered. I could still make out the high land on each side. The water was phosphorescent and each time I dipped the oars in, it coloured to a brilliant light green. It was as though the fishes had gone all electric below the surface.

I pulled into the cove just as Leo, looking like a biblical figure, was coming down the path holding up a lantern. His hair looked very wild, eyebrows blacker than ever and the sea-boots went scrunch as they reached the cove. Someone to reckon with. 'I could be frightened of you' I thought, carefully shipping the oars.

He came forward to take the painter. "Thank God you're back. Hell, I've been worried about you. What happened? No don't tie her up, I want to put her on a trip. You be going on up."

Choo-i had come down to greet me, hoping for a fish. I picked him up and carried him back to the hut. To my surprise I found the cosy stove had been lit. I sat down in front of it with Choo-i on my lap. I was puzzled. Why had Leo looked so wrought? I hadn't come back at an unreasonable hour.

Presently he joined us.

"I thought it had turned chilly so I got the fire going" he said, and gave it a poke.

"I'm sorry if I worried you" I said, "but I really didn't think I was terribly late.

He sat down with a heavy sigh.

"You're quite right. It's not very late. I'm a bit of an old fusspot aren't I? I'm always on edge when anyone's out at night with the boat. Can't settle to anything either 'til they get back. Never mind. Tell me about the dance."

I didn't feel inspired to do so for he seemed depressed. It wouldn't be tactful to tell him too much, or repeat the things Colin had said. So in a nonchalant tone, I just said that it hadn't been bad really, just a hop you know; and most hops are the same aren't they; and by the way did he know there was a jolly girl staying at the pink cottage with some friends?"

"I believe they are here for some time" I added, "and it might be nice for you to have semi-neighbours."

The thought of jolly neighbours did not raise his spirits either. I was growing anxious about the thought of telling him about the fun to come.

"I did a bit of work on **The Golden Waterwheel** this evening" he said "and I've been reading through some of the early chapters. It's damn good; some of my best writing there."

"I'd like to read them Leo."

"No, let me read it out loud, it helps me that way. But not tonight. You'd best go to bed now, you must be tired. I read some of it to Shawn before he went to sleep. He liked it. Oh hell, I'm going to miss him when he goes....he *is* a lovely boy."

I realized then I was ridiculous, even a little vain, to imagine that Leo was feeling blue because I had been to a dance with a boy. It was more likely that he was pre-occupied with thoughts of Shawn. He loved his boy and he didn't know when he was going to see him again.

"Go to bed, honey." He was half asleep himself, one foot resting on the stove. "Go on, we'll talk in the morning."

"Listen to Choo-i purring" I said.

It was so cosy by the fire.

****

⇑ When I was '*Stepping Out*'

⇑ Sailing with Shawn

⇐ Doreen Sloane, Leo & me in July 1952

⇐ Our home
⇓

⇑ Our Wedding Day
February 5th 1955

On the river with
Leo and Mother ⇒

⇑ On the river with Selina

⇑ Selina on the Cove at
'Paradise Creek'

CHAPTER XII.

LIFE WITH LEO.

Quickly the days went by. Happy days. *Amanda* behaving herself although she always started better when I was not there. But she took us to some lovely places, Pridmouth, Coombe, or up river.

On Sundays Doreen joined us. There was much fun then. Shawn loved it. We found a sack and rolled him in it all the way down the lawn. He splashed us violently in the water, using his finger tips making hail stones, then scrambled into the boat and rowed off fast before we could catch him. He rowed like a lord above the waves, pursuing us wherever we went.

I hadn't told Doreen about the motorboat. Shortly after she arrived on foot via the Polruan Ferry she asked where Leo was.

"Down on the cove" I told her "scraping the barnacles off *Amanda's* bottom."

Leo was not working full out on his book while he had Shawn for the holidays but he liked to work for a couple of hours on it each day. Visitors were discouraged, although fans delighted him, but he let no one interfere with his writing.

Happily Shawn was a child who could always take himself off and find something to do. He would pull about in the boat for the sheer bliss of it. Loving the water, we would both row out to *Amanda* at her moorings in the deepest part of the creek and jump into the water from her deck. He was a very good swimmer. Next came diving. We practised from oil drums washed up on the shore and later from *Amanda*.

Sometimes the child would be troubled by his father,s eccentric appearance. "Gosh daddy, what funny socks!" These being an ancient fisherman pair that Leo flopped around in after removing his sea-boots. This nearly brought the socks off too, leaving the toe part limp and footless. Quite devoid of personal vanity he never gave his appearance a thought, except for special occasions; and he had smartened up that first time I met him. Otherwise he wore any old garment, the older the better. Much of his time was spent on the boats, tinkering with the engine, or digging for worms in the mud. Without changing his garb he would go straight across to Fowey to shop or call on a friend. Consequently he drew many a second look from holiday makers (the locals were used to him) who noted with disdain the oil-stained denims and the worn out jacket. The old rucksack on his back was the final outrage.

Some artists and writers deliberately wear scruffy clothes in order to appear bohemian. With Leo it was never a pose. He was too honest for that. The mud that got on his clothes was good, clean mud not to be compared with sweat or city grime. It was a pity that his weird get-up belied the fact that he was really a clean man who enjoyed his hot baths.

It was lucky for Shawn that his holiday coincided with Fowey's annual regatta week. To quote his own words, it was "a week of fun and niceness." here was yacht racing, both in and outside the harbour, rowing races up the river, the crowning of the carnival and fairy queen, followed by the floral dance through the streets. The highlight was the carnival itself. Perched on the railings outside the church Shawn's eyes sparkled as he watched the procession above the heads of the crowd, the carnival queen riding by on a float decked out in flowers, an enormous sea shell behind her; the silver bands, the little fairy queen smiling and waving, the decorated horses, trade vehicles and tableaux. There were the competitors in all manner of weird and wonderful fancy dress, walking along in procession behind the band. It was like a jubilee and coronation all in one and everyone was happy. The pubs were packed with people and you could hear them singing from quite far off.

A big attraction was the baking of a giant sized Cornish pasty. Slices were distributed free to all children in the town. This was followed by dancing and community singing on the Town Quay.

The climax of the week was a firework display after dark. No child could have been more excited watching it, than Leo was.

When I told Leo about the regatta fancy dress party he reared up like a thoroughbred horse.

"Oh hell. This means another late night." He scratched his head and started to walk about. The wrought look had come back.

"The tides are about as awkward as can be this week." He stopped to look out on the creek, rolling himself a cigarette for comfort. "It may mean leaving the boat at Brazen Island to keep her afloat. How long does the thing go on for?"

I hardly dared tell him.

"Well you see" I began, faintly "it's a bit late.... until two a.m." I nearly squeaked.

He heard alright.

"Oh my God...." He broke off in horror. "Now it means I'll have to wait up for you, I wont be able to settle until you're back. Just when I wanted to get on with the book."

"I can manage the boat alright, I know what to do."

"No it isn't that, but you know what I'm like when anyone's out late." The pacing continued.

I had a bright idea. "Suppose I stayed with Esme overnight? She says I'm always welcome. I could moor the dinghy there."

This revived him. He stopped still."Oh no, no, no. I must have the boat back here." More pacing and thinking. Then, in a quiet voice, "Alright honey. I'm sorry I went off the deep end. I get a bit keyed up when I've got a book on my mind. You go to your dance."

Suddenly he spun round.

"But for God's sake be back before two!"

****

"I wish I could go to the dance" said Shawn watching me as I was about to pull on my sea-boots.

We were in the big room and I was ready to set off in the boat which had been moored on a trip anchor round by the headland.

"Your turn will come one day." I held out my arms to him, and put on a funny voice.

"Little boy, may I have the pleasure?" He gave me a self- conscious chuckle and with much grace and gaiety he danced with me around the room.

"Bravo!" said Leo, clapping hard. Shortly after I broke off and flopped into a chair, while my partner capered solo.

"The tide is ebbing fairly fast" Leo told me, "so you had better get your boots on. I'll walk down with you when you're ready."

I was wearing a Tyrolean outfit, a ready made fancy dress. Just then there was a loud shout from the cove.

"HELP!"

"Gosh! What's that?" from Shawn.

"Sounds like someone in trouble!" We rushed to the window. Far out we could see a figure of a man in a boat standing up waving rather frantically. I thought that I recognized him.

"I think it's Colin." Shawn dashed out to see. Quickly I pulled on my boots.

"I have a strong suspicion what has happened" said Leo, following me down to the cove. He chuckled maliciously.

The voice called out again and was clear to us now.

"I'm stuck in the mud! Can you help? It's me, Colin."

"Stay where you are."

"I borrowed the club dinghy to fetch Stephanie" said Colin when we had approached as near as we could to him. "I had no idea about the the tides."

The boat was aground and he was totally surrounded by mud.

"I'm afraid you really are stuck aren't you?" said Shawn pleasantly.

Leo was well in charge.

"You will have to leave the boat, she'll be aground for ages now. You can get ashore if you step out where the clumps of sea-weed are, it's usually firm there with stones underneath."

Colin looked dubiously around him.

"I got stuck in the mud once and I nearly sank" said Shawn helpfully.

"Look" said his father "will you go up and get the spare pair of wellingtons for him? They're on the balcony."

No persuasion was needed for this important mission. The child ran off full speed.

"Maybe I can manage" said Colin who had taken off his shoes and was rolling up his trousers. Gingerly he put one foot over the side of the boat.

"No, not there!" Leo shouted "for God's sake don't step there!" But he stepped—just there. One foot already sinking into pale grey mud was recklessly joined by the other. Both legs were now submerged up to the knee.

"Oh dear" groaned Leo "why didn't you wait for the boots?" He was always trying to save people from calamities like this. Shawn, hurrying back with them stopped still at the sight of Colin.

"Gosh!" This was better than the carnival.

"Get back in the boat" said Leo taking the boots from Shawn and picking his way via the sea-weed, towards Colin.

Colin's feet made a squelching, gurgling noise as he laboured to extract them from the blancmange like mud. He then heaved and groaned back into the boat and began to wipe off the mud with a clean white handkerchief.

"I hope this will teach you to study the tides next time" said Leo who had been laughing to himself throughout the operation.

Life With Leo

"I most certainly will" said the poor boy now pulling on the gum-boots. He then made his faltering way to the shore, this time stepping where he was told. He went up to the hut, where Shawn, who had dashed on ahead, had the smug pleasure of showing a big boy where to get washed.

The splashes of mud on Colin's trousers had brushed off quite well and he had wisely left his fancy dress garb at the club. He was going dressed as a Cambridge Don.

Leo was going to look after the club boat and we could borrow his dinghy. When finally we were ready to set off he gave instructions about mooring.

"Use plenty of rope, for when you land you will be a distance from the steps. Take the long painter we use for the trip and tie it to the shorter one, then there will be enough to fasten to the railings. She ought to be afloat soon after twelve. Try not to be too late," he added to me.

Colin's spirits began to lift as we climbed into the boat. Could he row? He was sorry to have made such a fool of himself, he said. He should have thought about the tides, but never mind, all's well that ends well. He beamed at me across the oars, thinking of the fun to come.

I suppose I was partly to blame for what happened later on that night, although I had every intention of playing Cinderella. However, once we got inside the club and found it packed with people in all forms of fancy dress, with a smart band playing all the hits of the day, I lost all count of time. We soon joined the others and began to dance the night away.

****

It wasn't until the band struck up 'Goodnight Sweetheart' that I suddenly remembered. "Hey what's the time?" Colin looked at his watch. It was nearly two a.m.

"Oh dear, and I promised not to be late!"

With some difficulty I wove my way through the dancers and over to the balcony to look at the boat. Thank God she was well afloat at her moorings.

"I'll have to be going" I told Colin.

"Wait a minute, we must have the last dance."

I was picturing that biblical figure doing an anxious survey of the cove.

Colin held out his hand, "Come on." Everyone was on the floor. "It's so late now that a few more minutes can't make any difference."

He led me back. we moved slowly, like dreamers to the sweet senti mental tune. The lights dimmed. Couples danced cheek to cheek. Girls nestled against their partners' shoulders. Both of Colin's arms went around me. Then the lights went out altogether. A delighted murmur went round the room. Colin pulled me close to him and his head bent down to me. But at that moment the lights came full on again causing us to break away startled. We laughed to cover our confusion.

Together we went down to the boat. The tide had risen very high. I saw that it had come right over the rope where we had made it fast to the ladder. Crouching down, I plunged my arms down into the water to free the knot. "I've been thinking" Colin said, watching me, "I wonder if Mr. Walmsley really would give me a spot of advice. I am so awfully keen to write. Maybe if I were to walk over some time tomorrow, through the hills."

With the rope now cleared and in my hand, I looked up at him as he bent to take it from me. I suddenly felt that I wanted to see him again. I knew Leo was often approached by aspiring writers and that he wouldn't want his working routine upset. Colin held on to the boat while I stepped in.

"You could take a chance on him being in during the afternoon, although he does like to do something with Shawn, like taking him fishing....as long as you don't come in the morning."

"And you. Will you be there?" In the dusky light by the water's edge he looked very attractive. I reached for the oars. "Yes" I said, and smiled at him, "I think I will be there."

****

I did not enjoy the trip back. Those 'electric messages' had begun to reach me. It really was awfully late. A bit of wind had sprung up. I was having to pull more on my left oar to prevent the boat veering towards the harbour. Leo who studied the tides and weather would be aware of this. He's sure to be in a flap by now, I told myself, putting more pressure to the oars.

Pulling very hard, I came to the entrance to Pont Creek. I went round the bend (and thought of Doreen and our silly jokes) and found it easier now that I was out of the harbour. No time though, to reflect how beautiful it was , this phosphorescent water. But I would soon be home now.

I was approaching the little pink cottage when I heard voices and laughter. Suddenly, as though from nowhere, hands appeared on each side of the boat.

"Hello! Come and join us! We're having a super swim." The hands tipped the boat, sending it rocking from side to side.

"OOPS!. Careful! She's nearly in!" I steadied myself with some alarm. A lantern, shining from the slipway, gave enough light to recognise a face. Beaming at me from the water was the jolly faced girl I had met before and a couple of men with beards. They had all been at the club. None of them appeared to be wearing bathing suits.

"We could have given you a tow back with our boat " said the girl. "We have an outboard motor. You're staying with Leo Walmsley and his son aren't you? We've seen you out with them in the blue motorboat. I was hoping I would get to know you soon."

About a dozen people were on the slipway, all in fancy dress and making plenty of noise. Some sat dangling their feet in the water.

"Do come in" coaxed the girl "Take your things off....it's simply super."

"Nothing like a swim in the altogether!" shouted one of the beards, rocking the boat violently so that I lurched and clutched the sides.

"Oh don't" I cried, but laughing so as not to seem stuffy. "I might fall in. Please, I have to be back."

"What for?" said the rocker "Back for what?" They were all a bit tipsy.

"Stop it boys!" shouted the girl.

"It's considered impolite" said the other beard, ignoring her, and bringing his full weight to bear down heavily on one side so that the boat all but toppled over. I screamed and held on frantically.

"Impolite" he continued, "to refuse so cordial an invitation."

After that I was given a short respite while the jolly girl, amid shrieks and yells, was ducked and held under. I shuddered at the memory of a similar thing happening to me at school when I was five. The girl, now released, came struggling and spluttering furiously up to the surface. She regained her breath and began splashing the others with full force. Watching them, I was unprepared for the next sudden onslaught. The boat was seized and was now being pushed and rocked in all directions at once, until down one side I went and....SPLASH! I was in.

I came up gasping, hair clinging to my face. Shrieks of laughter in my ears, the cold shock....and my nice frock. There were cries of "You shouldn't have done that John....beastly of you....just look at the poor girl." I was swimming about in circles like a crazed fish.

"Look out! One of the oars has fallen in." It was floating nearby and I made a quick grab for it.

"I say, are you alright?" said a voice with overtones of guilt.

"We can help you back in."

I had partly recovered from the rude shock, when the jolly girl swam towards me.

"I do hope you're not upset....it was very naughty of them." She cast a glance in the direction of the beards. "That's John, my husband, the one that pushed you" she added. "Cheers" said John, sheepishly. "And that's Paul, a friend who is staying with us....he's an artist." "Hi" from Paul. "I'm called Penny and we're renting the cottage for the summer. What's your name?"

"Stephanie."

"Once you're in it's quite fun don't you think?" said the friend lying on his back and kicking like a baby.

I had to agree for the water didn't seem cold anymore. I quite enjoyed splashing about with this lively trio.

"We're having a sort of party" said Penny "Such fun. You must meet the others. They're cheats not coming in." I swam a few more strokes then they helped me back in the boat. Dripping with water like some shaggy dog, I rowed to the slipway towing the others who clung on to the sides. There I made fast to a ring. John called out, "Meet Stephanie, she's just fallen in."

"Well I like that! You mean you tipped me over!"

"Did he really?" said one of the party " John! You rotten so and so."

There followed much horseplay between the slipway and the water. The two men shouted for towels to wrap round them and these were deliberately withheld, which provoked splashing reprisals from the water.

"Hey, you lot, chuck me my wrap from the rail will you?" shouted Penny, standing up to her waist in water. More horseplay. Now a pantomime of pretending to throw the garment into the creek. She finally caught it and wrapped it around her as she appeared on the slipway. "I don't know what you must think of us all" she said, "Here, come on up and I'll give you some things to put on." In the light of the lantern I saw that she was pretty in a plump, pleasant sort of way. Her eyes were shining with the joy of life.

"It's alright, I've haven't far to go."

"But you're soaking! Come and get dry and have a drink. We've got some super food laid on too."

Life With Leo

I accepted her offer of dry clothes as I was shivering a bit. The men had finally been given their towels and we all walked up to the bright cottage. Lights were on everywhere. Stepping inside I saw a cosy room with a handful of people all making themselves at home. There was an upright piano in the corner and someone was prodding the keys with one finger. Then I was led to a bedroom and given a sweater and a pair of jeans. I felt good after I had put them on. When I joined the party Penny gave me a glass of something hot.

"Gluwein" she told me " We had it in Austria last Christmas. It warms you up." I took a grateful sip. She was right. I felt it beginning to warm me right through. I took another sip. I mustn't have too much I told myself, beginning to giggle, or I'll see two biblical figures patrolling the cove.

I told Penny about my predicament, but she only thought it terribly funny.

"You have a good excuse. You capsized! Now you can stay a bit longer."

"Where did she come from?" said a lean girl in a Scottish kilt who was sitting slouched on the floor by the wall, "I don't recall seeing her before."

"She's been washed up" said a wit, "or rather she was pushed overboard."

Penny called out, "Meet Stephanie" and disappeared from the room. She returned with a large tray of Cornish pasties which she handed round. I took one. They were piping hot.

"Do you like the wine?" she asked me.

"It's lovely. I like the cinnamon flavour, and as for these pasties they're really special....still, although it's kind of you to want me to stay, I really must get back."

"Oh you can't possibly go yet." She topped up my drink.

"The road to hell" said John coming in, having got dressed "is paved with good intentions."

I'll go back as soon as I've finished this, I told myself, knocking back more of the cinnamon wine. My head swam a little and my heart was light.

A man in the guise of an Elizabethan sat down at the piano. He wore a full sleeved blouse under a suede tunic. The costume suited his aesthetic face. He began to play with great feeling and skill, some classical music, including Bach's 'Sheep May Safely Graze'. After that everyone clapped and I went over to congratulate him. Then he gave us a selection from 'The Beggars Opera' and Penny, in a sweet soprano voice sang 'Youth The Season Made For Joy'.

Autumn Gold

The party was well away, fast turning into a musical evening. Everyone wanted a go at the piano, even those limited to 'Chopsticks' with one finger. I was no exception and when it was free I played some Schubert pieces.

"That's Lilac Time" said Penny with her lighting-up smile. She hummed the melody. Next we sang 'Many A New Face' from Oklahoma, and songs from Carousel.

Someone called for dance music. Chairs were pushed back. The lean girl in the kilt got up, did a few steps of the Highland Fling, and finished up on the floor again.

Several people had a go after that. Some recited comic verses, others tried standing on their heads (some succeeded) and Penny did the splits. We all cheered her. I felt carefree and happy and I got up and did a tap dance. It went down well and I got a clap for it. The thought of getting back had left my mind for the present. I might have stayed out if I hadn't heard someone talking about a boat. I was brought back to earth with a jolt.

How loath I was to leave such gaiety and revelry and pressure was put on me to stay. However, the thought of Leo's wrought face and the times he must have been down to the cove, spurred me on. I managed to extricate myself from these new, fun, friends and after snatching up my soaking frock, I all but ran down the slippery slope. Penny followed and saw me off with a kindly shove.

"You will be in the dog-house when you get back won't you?" She was grinning gleefully, "Leo will be chucking a wobbly or something."

"He is sure to be in a terrible state. I'm dreading it."

"Blame it on to us."

"Anyway thanks for all the fun. I have enjoyed it."

A sudden thought struck her. "I know what, we'll all come over tomorrow."

I pulled hard on the oars.

"I'd like to meet Leo" she said, raising her voice as I was nearly out of sight "So would John. Cheerio for now."

"So long!" I called, a bit uncertainly, and lost her behind the jutting headland.

My heart was sinking as I approached the cove. The tide had come right in, hard to believe that a few hours ago there had been grey mud. All was ominously quiet, save for the lapping of the water against the steps.

Sick with guilt, I got out. With the smaller rope in my hand I made fast to the pulley and began paying out. This lovely smell of honeysuckle, it was everywhere.. I took a deep breath. Then, like a fugitive I walked up the steps.

The light of the lantern shone out from the balcony. Halfway up the path I was spotted, for suddenly I heard a shout. I nearly dropped the boots I was carrying. Then a voice called out in tones of almost wild alarm:

"IS THAT YOU STEVEY?" The anxious figure was on the balcony.

I replied "Yes" in a very small voice and as I reached the hut I was confronted with a stricken face looking down at me over the railings.

"THERE you are! By God.... What on earth.... What happened? Christ I've had a hell of a night. Do you know how late it is? I've been so worried about you."

I started to explain but he cut me short.

"Have you fixed the boat?"

"I let her out the whole length like you said." He hadn't noticed my change of clothes. As we went indoors I said, "I'm so sorry to come in at this hour, but I can explain...."

"I couldn't think what happened to you....I was just about to call round to those people you spoke of. Hell, I've been nearly off my rocker."

Then he noticed. "You're wearing a different outfit aren't you? You didn't go off in those togs. And your hair's wet."

"I fell in."

"You WHAT!"

"Fell overboard. I was pushed, I mean the boat tipped up."

"Good Lord. How did it happen?" I told him, adding afterwards, "It's a good job I can swim, isn't it?" I waited for his expression to change from outrage to sympathy, but he just looked exasperated.

"Damn fool thing to do. They didn't overturn the boat did they?"

"No they rocked it."

"Silly devils. That oar might have been lost. I'd better go and see if anything's missing."

He hurried down to the cove. When he came back he looked reassured. All was intact. "And you're alright, that's the main thing. I'm glad you brought my boots back." He sat down with a sigh of relief. "You haven't told me the rest of the story, what happened after your baptism?"

I got a towel from the rail to dry my hair and then sat on the floor by the stove. Leo took the towel from me and began to rub my head. It was a nice sensation, reassuring and protective. "You do want looking after" he said.

I thought then that I would like to be looked after by him.

Soon I was telling him the whole story. He listened intently. Now and again a wary look crossed his face when he heard of the antics of his new wild neighbours, although he wanted to know if Paul was able to sell his paintings.

"And how about your pretty boy?"

"Umm? Who?"

"The nice looking lad from Cambridge, did he enjoy himself?"

"Oh I see....Colin....yes he did."

"You haven't fallen for him have you?"

I turned round to look at him. "No I haven't. It's just nice to have some-one to go dancing with."

"He's young like you, and good looking. He's got everything I haven't got."

"But he can't write books like you, although he wants too." There was a pause.

Then, "He looked a poor fish after he got stuck in the mud" chuckled Leo with obvious relish. He was happy now savouring the memory of that mud spattered rival. He sat back in his chair, one foot on the stove, benign once more.

The following day I thought it best to warn Leo early of the approach-ing invaders. It was warm and sunny. I plunged straight in after breakfast with, "Oh by the way, Colin wants to come over this afternoon."

A moment's silence, then the stone fell. "Oh dear God." This was ut-tered softly, giving more impact. Exasperated, he felt in his pockets for his cigarettes. I've done it now, I thought.

"It won't be until this afternoon and he may...." My voice trailed off without conviction.

"Hell!"

"Why, what's wrong?"

"It's going to be every afternoon now, for this next week too.... my last with Shawn and you."

"What is?"

"He'll be here all the time."

"I don't think so, he wants to see you about something he has written. He is very keen to write and wants your advice."

This was received with half a smile. "Tell him to read my books. Has he read any?"

Leo was standing in characteristic pose, one arm tucked underneath the other.

"Yes. *Three Fevers*. He loved it." One up to Colin.

"Well I'll certainly try to help him if he is trying to write, poor fish. What time does he want to come?"

"I suggested the afternoon, and also Leo...."

"He'll make his own way?"

"Yes. Through the hills.... and Leo, those neighbours in the pink cottage." I cleared my throat, "They want to come too....They want to meet you."

Luckily before the rocket could go off, Shawn burst into the room.

"Guess what I've done!" he cried excitedly, "I've got a surprise for you Daddy," and he began to babble away. It was a most agreeable surprise. He had been out to *Amanda* and tidied her from top to bottom, washed her, scrubbed the deck and put all the tools away neatly. His eyes sparkled with pleasure, and he pulled his father's arm. "Come and see what I've done, come on."

Leo looked down at his son with amused affection. He was touched and his good humour restored. This promised well for the afternoon.

"You must keep her like that Daddy" said the child, "although," he added as the pair went down to the water, "I don't suppose you will for long."

It did not take me long to discover that Leo had a strong, built-in sense of self-preservation. He was a one-man protection society. Visiting friends who threatened to outstay their welcome had their departure hastened in various and often cunning ways. "Look the tide's ebbing, I'll have to take you back before the boat goes aground," or simply "Well I'm going fishing now so I'll drop you off at the Town Quay. Are you ready to go?"

They were never allowed to interfere or prevent him carrying out his jobs. If worms had to be dug, he dug them; or water to be pumped, he pumped it. Furthermore he inveigled their help and got them working. Often, an unsuspecting visitor, happily sipping a drink of tea, would be hustled down to the cove and asked to give a hand pushing the boat off. And they respected him for it.

Coming from a family who were inclined to treat guests with something like reverence, this was change for me. It was so different from my childhood days when mother would tell me to 'answer the door prettily to our guests...show them in graciously.' Leo's form of greeting was briefer, more to the point.

"Give me a hand with the coal will you, it's damned heavy."

Colin arrived nicely to give a heave up with the calor gas and the jolly neighbours who had brought their two small daughters with them, were quickly enticed into helping to turn the dinghy upside down for minor repairs. On the whole Leo made the best of it and reconciled himself to a lively afternoon. I won't say that he did'nt enjoy himself discussing his books and showing them his paintings, for they were admiring and attentive.

After a scathing look at the little girls, Shawn felt it was beneath his dignity to make overtures to them. Eight does not mix with four and six. The fact that they were females damned them from the start and labelled them 'wet' and 'weedy'. He was'nt going to be lumbered with them for the afternoon! Before we had a chance to ask him to take them for a row, he had climbed into the boat and, with a proprietary air, was pulling about in all directions at once, showing off like mad while they stood in silent admiration by the water's edge. Next they were treated to a demonstration of his new skill, swimming and diving off petrol cans. After this he did his best to ignore them.

We had caught some prawns earlier on and had them for tea that day. We made a driftwood fire on the cove and cooked them in saltwater from the creek. They went down very well with plenty of bread and butter.

After that there was a standing invitation to call on the jolly neighbours at any time - open house - they said. Like Leo, all their shopping was done by boat so we often passed them on the water. Sometimes while Leo and Shawn were out fishing, or making something in the workshop, I would go round and see them. They usually had several others there as well, for they loved to fill the house with people. Knowing that Leo did not, we used it for our rendezvous. Colin was also given a big welcome and many happy hours were spent swimming, fooling about, and drinking numerous cups of tea and coffee.

It was nearing the end of the holiday. I could sense Leo's sadness. It would be a long time before he would see his boy again.

An old song kept running through my head and I sang it sometimes on our long walks or when we were in the boat.

Life With Leo

What will I do when skies are grey
and you are far away.
What will I do?

Shawn soon picked it up and whistled or sang it cheerfully, unaware of the pathos. Even the seagulls seemed to take up the melancholy theme.

Apart from our own creek there were one or two others, Lerryn being one of the most beautiful. The entrance to Lerryn lay up-river beyond the station and jetties, and past the waterside village of Golant. It had its own regatta (a miniature Henley some called this) which included mud races, competitions and a fair. People sat on the river banks watching the fun while the fairground music blared out. It was always held to coincide with the right tides, so those going by boat, the loveliest way, went up on the flood and returned on the ebb.

One afternoon we cruised up Lerryn creek and had a picnic on one of the banks. As usual we took the old black kettle and we took winkles, prawns, watercress sandwiches and a jam sponge that I had made.

There was something in the air that day, apart from the first hint of autumn, something not quite tangible, but it was there. Already the green leaves were darkening to gold and there were early morning mists. But it was something more than that, otherwise why do I remember it so vividly, as though it were yesterday.

Amanda was behaving nicely. The mooring was easy as Leo simply made fast with the rope to an anchor and carried it ashore. All the pleasure boats were out carrying loads of happy people. There were hired motor-boats, rowing boats and privately owned craft, and they all went at a leisurely pace, for why hurry on this lovely summer's day? Supine forms stretched out on the decks of their cabin cruisers, their bodies covered with glistening oil.

We spread out our feast on the grass and Shawn ran off to look for sticks to light a fire. He had become so tanned that he could have passed for a young West Indian or South Sea Islander. He was sparkling with health and vitality, his pocket full of plums.

Leo, sitting on the bank, was unravelling one of his fishing lines. Every so often he would look out at the enchanting scene, missing nothing, his eyes like a camera snapping up memories.

"I'll never forget this holiday with you and my boy" he said presently, "Hearing you laugh with him in the water, seeing the look in his eyes when he lands a fish, and I don't think he will after either. He dearly loves you. It thrills me to feel, that for a little while, you have shared my love for this kind of life, that you were able to enjoy the beauty of the creek with all its changing moods." I wanted to say I too have loved it Leo, don't think it's been all one sided, when he went on: "He's already gone you know. I put myself forward in time to when he'll be back home. A form of self protection I suppose."

Just then Shawn came hurrying back with his arms full of twigs, blissfully happy, living right in the present as children do.

"Look I've got masses" he cried, and dumped them all down on the ground. "Shall we swim before tea? we can jump off *Amanda*. Daddy is it deep enough? Will I sink in the mud?" But there was plenty of water as the tide was still flowing. I dived in with him and we swam in the placid water. It was so warm, like being in a bath. Like thirsty drinkers we could not have enough of it. Each time we came ashore the hot sun dried us so quickly that we were hot again, so it was back on *Amanda* and into the water once more.

A few yards down river a couple were in a boat that was moored with a line overboard. They didn't seem bothered if they caught a fish or not. The man was reclining astern, a straw hat pulled down over his eyes. Every now and then he gave a lazy jerk to the line while the woman sat amidships gazing contentedly ahead of her and eating food taken from a hamper on her lap.

How many people, at some point in their lives must have wished for time to stand still. I know I did on that day on the shores of Lerryn creek. We stayed there a long time, until most of the pleasure boats had gone back, until the heat had gone from the sun and it had begun to set, a great ball of orange in the sky.

I looked down at the water. It reflected the green of the trees above the banks. Every so often there came a movement, a ripple, showing clearly that the fish had come in on the tide. "We ought to get any amount on the way back" said Leo, "You'd better each have a line." Then with a sigh he said "Come on, time to pack up."

He put some heaped up leaves on the fire, which like our holiday, was dying out.

"I don't want to go home" said Shawn suddenly. He had come to watch his father. I looked at him, this lovely boy with the dusky skin and large dark eyes. In one hand he had a slice of cake and his skin was smudgy with plum juice. I wondered if I would ever see him again in the future, and I too gave a sigh. Soon I would be joining my fellow actors and he would be back at school.

Nothing stays, I thought, watching the blue smoke from the fire. Time was like quicksand, you could not hold it, it just ran out.

****

CHAPTER XIII.

ON WITH THE SHOW.

At first it took me a while to get used to being back with the company. I was so full of the holiday, still absorbing the atmosphere of that enchanting place, the hut and the huge sunflowers growing against it, the sloping lawn, the watercress stream, the beauty of the creek and the smell of wild honeysuckle which grew by the cove. In my mind's eye I could see the barefoot boy running down to the cove see his father hauling in the nets.

In many ways it was nice to be back at work and to see Doreen again. There was so much to tell her. We talked for hours. Our repertoire had increased alarmingly and I would have to work hard to catch up. I thought I saw a glint in her eye at this.

So it was on with the tour, let joy be unconfined. I returned in time to travel with the company from Dingle to our new destination, a village called Harebell. It was about six miles away in the heart of the china clay country, the chief industry there being tin mining.

"So you had a good holiday then?" said Tony, raising his eyebrows at me as we lurched and bumped along in the van.

"Yes very good" I told him, feeling a bit guilty at taking a month off from the hard slog. I felt a cross between the prodigal son and a deserter from the army as I met the stares of Brenda and old Mrs. Howard.

Robbie in his strong Sottish accent said "Well lass, you picked a fine time to take a holiday in all this fine weather didn't you?"

After we had arrived at the village we had to set about finding accommodation, for Joe as well as us this time. Doreen and I had once again to traipse round from door to door like commercial travellers. We plodded on for some time searching for signs saying Bed and Breakfast, but we couldn't see any. I grew despondent.

"We may end up at the Police Station."

"Or worse, in the van. Having to kip down with all the others."

"And eat fish and chips sitting on the floor." This thought spurred us on and we quickened our step. "What I could do with a plate of fish and chips right now" said Doreen.

We had tramped on a few hundred yards more when we came across a wonderfully large lady, all floury from baking, who was about to enter her house from the grocer's shop adjacent to it. "Let's go and ask her" I said, feeling bold. The door was half open and wafting from within there came a lovely smell of home cooking. Perhaps it was a case of needs must, or maybe we just had colossal cheek, for there was no accommodation sign, but on the principle that a bit of cheek may get you somewhere we approached her and came straight to the point.

"Excuse me" I began, "but we're looking for somewhere to stay."

"And we wondered if you do bed and breakfast," said Doreen, "Or perhaps full board," she added faintly. That's pushing it a bit I thought and went on to tell her about Joe. The lady, who had a round pink face, looked kind but she eyed us with suspicion. She wiped her hands on her apron and said she would have to confer with her husband who was serving in their shop next door.

"Lovely jam tart lady, take us in" I said beseechingly, after she had gone.

"Take us to your bosom" said Doreen.

"No, your larder!"

She returned presently with a mild-faced man of small stature. Luck was on our side. We were in.

Smiling at us and speaking with a soft Cornish accent, the man said that though they did not normally do this sort of thing, they would make an exception for us. He might have added that they were not used to total strangers presenting themselves out of the blue and asking for bed and board. As for the young man, they thought they could find a room for him but would naturally like to meet him first. Meanwhile if we would come inside his wife would see to us. Their name was Bacon, he added.

"Can't get away from food for long can we? "murmured the hungry Doreen. We followed the lady into a pleasant living room where we discussed terms.

It was a nice house, small and compact and in a short time we were all siting around the table, Joe too, tucking into hot Cornish pasties, fruit pie and cream.

We opened our first week at the village hall with **Maria Martin** or **Murder in the Red Barn**, a creepy, shuddering melodrama that had you in its grip from the start. Doreen played Maria and I was Nan, her sister. I loved my part. I loved going stealthily across the stage to where old Mrs. Howard sat 'sleeping' in a rocking chair, tugging her sleeve and saying in urgent tones '*Mother, wake up, I've had a terrible dream....wake up mother....I dreamt that our Maria has been murdered in the red barn!*' We played this scene in front of the curtain with dimmed lights; you could feel the audience nicely squirming in their seats and I knew that they were going to love being scared. They shouted 'BOO' when the baddies came on which created the right atmosphere. We were like the barn-stormers of bygone days. The play was so popular, with the hall packed out each night, that Tony decided to keep it going for a week.

"This has always gone down well with them, " said Mrs. Howard, whose experience as a travelling player spanned over fifty years. She always referred to the audience as 'them' or 'out front'. She didn't seem unduly elated by the success of the play - she had been at the game too long now. It was just a question of survival. They would eat well this week.

"You done a good job there you girls, Joe too" said Mrs. Bacon after the show that night. "We were around the table having a late supper. Both she and her husband had been to see the play and they were full of it.

"'Twas like as though it were really happening, eh Percy?"

"Sure enough" said Percy, who never said much.

"'Pon my soul! It do make my flesh creep just thinking of it. And some packed out in there 'twas too. They had we gripping our seats didn't us Perce?" ·

The following day Tony hurled a batch of exercise books at me with orders to get cracking. In them was a variety of parts to learn. The first of these was 'Baby' in a play called **Spring Meeting**. The character was whimsical and a bit twee. I had little idea what the play was about, as there was only my part written out as usual by Mrs. Howard, with just the barest cue preceeding my lines.

At the time of my story, the permissive society had not been heard of. There was still a guide line, a code for living. I wasn't blind to the fact that however innocent the holiday had been, my staying over there must have caused some speculation. It did not bother me too much, although I liked to be well thought of by the Cornish people, especially those I became involved with, like our landlady. She was both kind and good natured. She also had a conventional outlook, and I learned this during a short conversation we had while I was trying to learn my lines. I was sitting at the table with my exercise book in front of me and she had come into the room to lay the tea.

"I see you'm busy so I won't disturb 'ee m'dear" she said, putting a tray of crockery on the table.

"Can I help?"

"No, you stay where you are, I'll be back directly." All the same I put things around. Presently she returned with another tray loaded with sandwiches and cakes. Putting out the food, she asked why I was the only one working. I explained about my 'working' holiday.

"So you've been up the creek for a while! And this gentleman, he do live up there?"

"Yes."

"Summer and winter?"

"All weathers."

"Get away!"

"He lives all alone except when his little boy comes to visit him."

"There now,'tis lovely for him I reckon."

"Oh yes, he looks forward to it all the year. The little boy loves it there."

"Dear of him too."

"He's so handsome, I've never seen a boy like him."

"There....and you've known Mr.Walmsley some time?"

"Mr.Walmsley? no, I only met him a few weeks ago." A stunned silence after this while I could almost hear her thoughts buzzing. Having by now made the table look most appetising, she went to the door and stood watching me for a while as I resumed my study. Then she said that she didn't think that life up the creek would suit her and Percy. She liked to be able to pop over to the shops when she felt like it and talk to a body. "And it must be some quiet in the evenings, no it wouldn't do for we" she said.

I suddenly thought of those evenings, the quiet contentment I had known for that brief time, and I realised how much I had loved it there. When she had left me I closed my eyes for a second, and vividly, I saw the hut, the garden and the cove, and heard again the soft lapping of the water against the boats.

Was I falling in love with Leo I wondered? I had always found older men more attractive than boys. Boys were awkward with their Adam's apples and their breaking voices. Raw youth. That is how I saw them. I remember as a child having a crush on our handsome village doctor. He bore a slight resemblance to film star Gary Cooper and shared the same surname; always if he was driving by in his car and saw my sister and me out walking, he would solemnly raise his trilby hat to us. That had been wonderful. Later in adolescence we fell in love with Gary Cooper and Fred

Astaire.

Although he bore no resemblance to Gary Cooper or Clark Gable, Leo was attractive. I had seen photographs of him in his younger days looking so strikingly handsome that he might have been mistaken for the actor Ronald Coleman. Maybe I just had a juvenile crush on an older man, who for me had a strong charismatic personality.

The following morning brought a letter from Leo, joyous, spontaneous, lighting up the day. I read it eagerly stretched across the bed. Then I read it again and went to show it to Doreen and read it all over again with her. This was the letter:-

Darling Stephanie,

Thank you for coming into my life, making me laugh, dance and live again, yes and love again.

It was the happiest of all my holidays with Shawn. You were just wonderful with him and I just pray that you have joined us for all holidays in the future.

> *I can't put what I feel into words....*
> *And now to WORK - and to count the days to Sunday!*

Leo.

I knew then that I would always keep that letter. I suddenly felt terribly happy.

"Doreen I do love it here" I said, "I love Cornwall and I love being with this crazy rep. outfit even though it will never get us anywhere, but it's all so mad and such fun."

Doreen, grinning like the Cheshire cat said she too was terribly happy, and she too loved Cornwall, and the people in Harebell and "I'm terribly glad that I answered that ad. in 'The Stage' magazine aren't you? We're always laughing aren't we?"

"Yes, and in all the wrong places sometimes, like the other night when you were lying 'dead' on the floor. I saw your chest heaving quickly up and down and when the curtains drew across and left you visible to the audience I nearly exploded."

"Imagine that happening in a real theatre! I'm glad we're going down so well here. They really love the play don't they, and it was a full house again last night."

"Mrs. Bacon is such a character. "Oi do dearly love a boil m'dear, but oi wouldn't give 'ee a thank you for a fry up!"

"She feeds us like fighting cocks. You should have heard what she said to me yesterday; "Oi do suffer something terrible with the wind m'dear, it do go rolling about inside me at night like thunder."

"Funny, I thought I heard a loud thump last night. Poor Percy! Perhaps he got blown out of bed!"

And we laughed down the stairs to breakfast.

Mrs. Bacon was already at the table with Joe, eating porridge and pushing the cream towards him. Percy was serving in the shop.

"Come on Joe, take more than that boy - why you'm thin enough, nothing of 'ee I reckon."

Doreen did not need any persuading.

We discussed the play.

"Tony could risk keeping it on for a further week I think."

"I hope he does, I love playing in melodramas."

"How are you getting on with your part in **Spring Meeting**?" Joe asked me, "The girl who took your place while you were away played it."

"Did she do it well?"

"Yes I thought so."

"You like her don't you?" said Doreen, "He took her to the cinema one day" she added to me.

"There now" said Mrs. Bacon, almost triumphantly. She was following our conversation with her eyes, watching us intently. "So Joe's got himself a bit of skirt!" Joe went red and coughed.

"Look at him blushing" said Doreen. "He actually had a bath before he took her out."

"Aw pack it up will you?" said Joe.

"Don't you stand for it Joe" said Mrs. Bacon, laughing. She felt obliged to stick up for him as he came in for a lot of ragging.

"By the way" said Doreen to me, "You have to have an Irish accent. She's got the lead next week" she added for Mrs. Bacon's benefit.

Luckily I was strong on accents as I had been born with a gift for mimicry.

"She's a winsome character, the heroine, isn't she. Whenever I get the lead I seem to wind up with something a bit twee."

"Fey is a better word" said Doreen "which suits you because you are a bit."

"And the word for you will be fat if you eat any more cream!"

If one of us dried up in a scene and was not responding to the fierce prompting of Mrs. Howard, she would resort to her old stand-by, the vase of flowers. These, a bunch of plastic tulips were kept ready in the wings. Summing up the urgency of the situation she would flash out a command to anyone nearby, "Take on the flowers QUICK!" This awful job some-times fell to me. Hastily grabbing the flowers, and often with a push from the old lady, I would have to go on and ad-lib. It didn't seem to matter what gibberish I came out with so long as I said something. In a light comedy it would be safe to come out with something like, "I always think flowers brighten a room." This would bring a look of anguished gratitude from the wretched actors struggling with their scene. It gave them temporary res-pite, but did not always set them back on their course. If the silence pre-vailed, Mrs. Howard would hiss at me "KEEP TALKING - go on, SAY ANYTHING."

In **Spring Meeting** I had a scene with Tony where I kept drying up. I decided to take no chances. It would be fatal if Doreen had to take the flowers on. So after getting her to hear my lines for the hundredth time I suddenly thought of a secret remedy.

The scene took place on a settee and I would be wearing a short sleeved frock otherwise my plan would not work.

It was a regular habit now for Mrs. Bacon and Percy to come to our plays. They showed a lively interest in them and met all their friends in the audience.

"Good luck m'dear" said Mrs. Bacon as I prepared to leave for the hall in good time. "We'll be watching out for 'ee."

Not too closely, I thought, or you might get a surprise.

My plan worked beautifully. The play was received with much enthusi-asm, and I managed to keep my secret from my leading man as he was too wrapped up in his own part to notice.

I waited before telling the others, until we were all around the table at supper.

"I'm amazed you didn't dry up in that scene" said Doreen." I was keep-ing my fingers crossed.....the times I heard your lines and you still didn't know them."

"But you done well" put in Mrs.Bacon "A proper job that, eh Perce?"

" 'Twas 'andsome" said the loyal Percy.

On With The Show

"At last" I said "I can reveal my dark secret....Look," I thrust my arm across the table and showed them. All along the inside of my left arm I had written out, in careful print, those elusive lines that I had been unable to learn.

There were exclamations all round. (Although it did not come as a surprise to Doreen. She had done this trick before.)

"You artful thing!"

"Crafty I call it."

"Well, she fooled we alright."

I grinned at them. "Well, it solved a problem didn't it?"

I was not the only one taking a short cut to success. Often in this crazy outfit there would be a scene between two players where each anticipated the thoughts of the other so the dialogue was always in suspension. The result could be hilarious, and I wondered if such scenes had been cut out by Tony in order to make it easier to learn the lines. For the audience it was a case of having to read between them, but perhaps it wasn't difficult in a scene llike this:

"Madge , my mind is made up...." (Paces floor, arms behind back.)

"Arthur!"

"I'm afraid the time has come...."

"You mean you...."

"I'm afraid so....I can no longer...."

"Oh no Arthur, no...."

"Try to understand my dear. At the time I thought, I really thought...."

"That you....?"

"That we...."

"And now you don't?...."

"Not any more my dear....not any more."

Not only were liberties taken with plays but also with sex and age. Like the time I was cast as a boy and old Mrs. Howard had to play a man. It became too much when I found myself having to play her mother while she decked herself out in a flowery summer dress and summer hat.

There's no business like show business. We had to be able to do anything, often at the last minute, like sing a song or do a dance. Our repertoire now included shows like the **Jolson Story** and **Sonny Boy**.

"We have to be all-round artistes like they advertise in 'The Stage' I explained to Mrs. Bacon.

"I can't visualise old Mrs. Howard doing high kicks" said Doreen.

"Nothing would surprise me now, she's already played my teenage daughter and a hearty sergeant in the army."

"Poor ol' soul" said Mrs. Bacon.

"Perhaps Joe will be called upon to dance **The Dying Swan**."

"Aw bloomin' heck" groaned Joe, "You girls...."

"Joe's a very nice young man" said Mrs Bacon when he was out of earshot "and I do know for a fact that he do fancy one of 'ee, don't know which one 'tis, mind." It was a wonder he put up with us, the way we ragged him.

A good all-rounder in the show was Jimmy, a natural comic. We sometimes did sketches and comedy scenes and he never failed to draw laughs when he came on with a melancholy face, paused, and then began in his strong Scottish brogue:

"Ahm not well...Noo, ahm not reeght....Just been to the doctor, and he says ah've got the heebie jeebies...." The women in the audience especially loved old favourites like "Winter draws on dear lady" and sketches that mentioned vicars were a sure hit, like the one:

"May I offer you a tongue sandwich vicar?"

"No thank you dear lady, I never touch anything coming out of an animal's mouth."

"Well in that case we'll have to boil you an egg!"

It was good simple fun with not a trace of smut.

Life with the company was all a farce, the wild studying, the scanty rehearsals. It took me quite a time to learn the batch of new plays, but I managed to make a compromise. None of us could be word perfect in that outfit.

After a while my thought turned back to Leo and Fowey. I had written him a letter full of chat about the company and had received several more letters from him. He would keep Sundays for me, he said, the only day I was free, and I could bring Doreen. He was now back to his working routine on the book. Sometimes I went alone, while Doreen went out with Joe.

These Sundays became the highlight of my week. As I drew into Fowey I would see that faithful, eccentric figure at the bus stop looking out for me, anxious, eager, his hair wild, the old rucksack slung across his back. The boat would be moored at the Quay, and if it was raining he would offer me his duffle coat to wear going across, no matter how wet he became himself. He was so excited about seeing me. He had cooked the lunch himself with nice vegetables from the garden, but could I make custard for the fruit?

Afterwards we might have a trip in *Amanda*, out to sea fishing, to Golant, or up to Pont. Or we would just spend a very happy afternoon by the fire being cosy and warm while the rain lashed down on the corrugated roof.

The weeks went by, Autumn nearing Winter; the bracken was beautiful on the high land at Pont, here a darkening gold, now brown, now red. Some days the water was as clear as polished glass, the air soft and mild. On others there would be mists or tearing wind.

And still I went there, nearly every Sunday, except when I had to learn new plays from the repertoire.

"I can't think what she keeps going over there for" I overheard Mrs. Bacon saying one day "Some quiet it must be now....married man too and a great deal older than she. I wouldn't entertain it myself."

Sometimes it is hard to underdstand why people are drawn together. I could not explain it to her. "I think you'm just fascinated by Mr. Walmsley, that's what it is m'dear. You'd do better to look at Joe. And what about that nice young man that took 'ee out?"

'I feel so right with him,' I told myself. 'He gives me a feeling of peace.' I could be silent with him without awkwardness and above all he was the positive side to my indecisive nature. It was inevitable that I should be drawn to him, and as time went on I knew I would come to be lost without him.

During some of our walks together when we went up through the farmer's field, along the road to Lantic Bay (memories of Shawn and his bag of plums) or along the quiet lanes to Lanteglos, we discussed the repertory company and the merits of staying with them. Leo thought I would do better to have a shot at Windsor or Birmingham repertory.

"You'll have to take Stephanie Gubbins more seriously" he said. "The lovely line of least resistance....will you always be dancing along it, over the hills and far away?" It was perfectly true.

"From a selfish point of view though" he added "I'd rather you carried on with the present outfit, for if I thought I wasn't going to see you again I'd crack up completely." I took these words to heart and one afternoon, during a slack period without much studying, I went for a long walk to think things out.

Leo had been talking sense.

****

CHAPTER XIV.

MY GOLDEN CHANCES.

From the age of four I never had any doubt about wanting to go on the stage. I had been to dancing and drama school and had private lessons in tap dancing and singing. There had followed seasons in repertory, pantomime and plays on tour. Was it all to be thrown away?

I kept thinking of Leo's words, they came into my mind as I clowned and fooled about with Doreen, or waited in the wings for my cue. Life was precious. If we had any sort of gifts we must use them. I began to think of my life up until now. The chances I had had. Opportunity had knocked several times.

When I was very young I became infatuated with Noel Coward. I thought him witty, loved his songs, and to me he was the quintessence of theatreland; the land that had such appeal for me. I was fifteen when this magical thing happened. A letter came for me one morning. I knew it contained something nice. I paused before opening it to prolong the sudden joy I felt. Then I opened the big buff envelope and took out first a photograph and then a letter, written in a beautiful hand on elegant notepaper. It read:

Dear Stephanie Gubbins,

I hear a sinister report from John Gordon that you admire my works. I am very flattered by this and I am sending you a photograph as a souvenir.

If by any chance the whole thing is a vast fabrication, don't humiliate me by sending it back, but quietly and discreetly tear it up!

Yours sincerely

Noel Coward.

Stunned with joy I wrote back a rather gushing letter, which resulted in a meeting with this king of the theatre. It was not difficult to arrange for he was in a play at that time called 'Present Laughter' at the Haymarket. The manager of the theatre, Jack Watson, was friend of family. "Be sure" he cautioned, as he took me round himself to the Lions' dressing room one evening after the show, "not to get up on a chair and sing or recite something."

I could hardly speak with excitement let alone sing.

Along we went, through a corridor, down a lush green carpeted staircase to a door on which was written 'Mr. Noel Coward'. A gentle knock, and at once it was opened by an obsequious manservant. There, splendidly attired in a red and white spotted dressing gown was the object of all my thoughts and dreams. He came floating towards me with outstretched hands, seized one of mine in both of his own and pressed it warmly, keeping it there for some sweet, giddy seconds while my head began to swim and my feet hardly touched the ground.

"How sweet of you to come" he said, still keeping my hand. Please keep holding it, I thought, hardly able to believe that life could suddenly bloom so rich and colourful. How fiercly then I wished for time to stand still, that my hand might ever be a happy prisoner in both of his. But it was returned to me, gently, and we talked, or rather he did. He told me he loved my father's writing "He's my Sunday joy. I adore him, he's so scathing."

As he spoke I took in every detail, the strangely bright blue eyes, the peach tan of his theatre make-up. His hands were slim, artistic and I noticed some little scars over his cheeks. I would not have cared if he had been covered in them, so mad about him I was then.

And then it came. The question every actress would dream of being asked by such a big star. We had been discussing the play he was in, it was autobiographical, and by coincidence one of the characters was a young girl called Daphne who was dotty on him, like me. He told me about a forthcoming tour and a new play he was going to write. I was drinking it all in when he suddenly asked: "And you? What are you going to do with your life?"

I gathered up my courage. Desperately I wanted to tell him. I wanted to say 'I'm training for the stage. One day, if I'm good enough I hope to have a small part in one of your plays'. He waited. It was a bitter-sweet moment for the words were slow to come. Finally he spoke for me: "You must write, like your Poppa." I missed a great chance there.

Two things you do not get back in a lifetime. The spoken word and the lost opportunity. And yet I must have been the exception for there were more chances just around the corner.

Before I left, and I think the Gods must have been smiling down on me that day, my idol asked me if I would like to wait and come along to the party. A NOEL COWARD PARTY!

What followed after that is like a hazy dream; then suddenly it was all happening and I was being led in on the arm of this theatrical giant to an enchanted room filled with flowers and bowls of cherries. Glamorous stars of the show-biz world stood chatting in groups, or moved about hailing each other and smiling brilliantly. There was music and soft lights and the fragrance of many kinds of perfume filled the air. As the beautiful people seemed to parade before my eyes I felt a sense of unreality as though I were watching it all from another planet.

Like a theatrical Who's Who, anybody who was anybody was there. My radiant host led me up to some of the great, saying: "Meet Ivor Novello... Let me introduce you to John Gielgud...Peter Ustinov."

Dazed by the scene I almost believed that I too was a V.I.P.

Certain impressions, snatches of conversations, these have stayed clear in my mind. They stand out like three dimensional pictures - that Ivor Novello was very handsome - that C.B.Cochrane, sitting down with a walking stick between his knees told me, "You're just like your mother my dear" - that Deborah Kerr's hair was a gorgeous red.

When my host vanished to mingle with his friends, the kindly manager of the theatre was never far away. As though still waiting to be roused from a dream, I would be lost among the cherries gazing at the splendour of the scene.

Later, while emerging from the cloakroom, this magical being spotted me and called in his clipped voice: "Little Gubbins come and meet John Mills."

I had a certain presence, even at that age as I was used to meeting colourful people at the parties my parents gave, and this gave me the nerve to confront Sir Michael Redgrave when I found myself standing next to him. He had his back against the long buffet table at the far corner of the dazzling room. The table was laden with delicacies of every sort including bowls of strawberries and jugs of cream. I was too excited to eat anything. Sir Michael looked rather aloof. Undaunted, and without a second thought I introduced myself quite boldly and said just what I had heard mother say to one of her friends.

"I simply loved **A Month in the Country**." (He was appearing in the play of that name at the time.) My words were received with a surprised stare, the ghost of a smile and an outstretched hand, then still staring, with eyes opening wide he shook my hand, thus jerking the cup of coffee I was holding and spilling some of it on my frock. His expression changed from surprise to mild horrror and he began to apologise profusely. This somehow balanced my colossal cheek in accosting him, and I felt we were quits.

What golden opportunities. Famous stars, producers, impresarios they were all there, as though the world of entertainment had come to me, been placed at my feet and having been presented with this gift I did not know how to use it. So nearly I might have been a star, so that I think there were conflicts in my nature, one urging me forward to the bright lights, the other beckoning me to the shadows to be a spectator.

If I had been too shy to answer Noel Coward's very direct question, opportunity knocked again, for some time after the party he sent me an audition card for a musical he was putting on. Apparently Jack Watson had told him that I was an aspiring actress.

Once again I was nearly there. No girl could have had more chances. But fate stepped in for by that time I had joined E.N.S.A before it folded up and had flown off to India in a touring revue.

uring that memorable tour another chance came my way. We had just left Calcutta having linked up with Ralph Reader's Gang Show, performing every night at the Garrison Theatre there. Bombay was the next stop, and shortly after we arrived, actor Jack Hawkins sent a message that he would like to see me. At the time he was the head of entertainment for South East Asia. In other words my boss. He was charming and asked me if I was happy in the show. I answered that I was, which was true in spite of the fact that we often had to rough it; working conditions could be grim out there. But we had the smooth as well as the rough and in Bombay we stayed at the Taj Mahal Hotel which was very swish indeed.

The E.N.S.A's company was not large. Just four girl dancers including myself and four men, a comedian, singer, drummer and pianist. Apart from a mad Russian dance which exhausted us in the burning heat, I enjoyed it all and I sang a duet with another girl. It was called 'Two Good Girls', a satirical number by Eric Spear who wrote some lovely music for the show and years later composed the theme for 'Coronation Street'.

My 'boss' then put the question to me. Would I like to join a company which was about to make a tour of Ceylon. They would be performing a number of fine plays under the direction of Roger Livesey and his wife Ursula Jeans, who were also in the cast. It would be a grand opportunity, he said. What did I think? He waited, smiling.

A jinx must have been on me that day. If only someone could have given me a big push.

I hesitated, turning it over in my mind. Then I thanked him and said that I was very grateful for the chance to join a crack company like that, but I was really sort of used to being with the present one, and I would miss the girls who were my friends. I didn't add that I was scared to accept the challenge wondering if I would be good enough to work with such fine actors. He must have thought me strangely unambitious

Still the chances came and it seemed that some force was driving me towards the glittering world of Noel Coward only to haul me back before I could get there. It drove again some years later after the India tour had finished. I was in a repertory company in the seaside town where I lived. We were doing **This Happy Breed** one week and Noel Coward, who had a cottage a few miles away came along to see his play. After the show he went backstage to congratulate the actors. And where was I that night? Off sick with the measles!

I decided that I must not waste any more time, but grab each chance as it came. There was no merit in staying with Howard Productions. It was just a great charade. If I was to forge ahead with my career it must be goodbye Cornwall and find myself some digs in London. I learned the hard way that in show business you have to be on the spot and must never be outside the radius. Jobs were lost through not being in the right place at the right moment.

However, some of my lost chances were not my fault, like the time I went along to see Sir Laurence Olivier about appearing in in the play **Skin Of Our Teeth**. He was producing it, and also starring in it with his beautiful wife Vivien Leigh. I met them both at the theatre. I remember how friendly they were, how warmly they smiled at me. Vivien Leigh was like a delicate little kitten and hardly weighed more than six stones. They were standing just beneath the stage. Sir Laurence asked me if I would like to just walk across it. The idea was for him to pick me up and hold me high above his shoulders. I managed the walking bit alright, but sadly, I was not of the same cast as Vivien Leigh. Not that I was big, just a medium eight stones but not light enough to be swung up that high.

"Sorry dear" said Sir Laurence, "I would have liked to offer you the part otherwise."

He looked so handsome with a rose in his buttonhole. Vivien Leigh smiled sympathetically at me.

Another plum that was dangled in front of me was the part of 'The Sugar Plum Fairy' in a pantomime up north. I went to see a theatrical agent who supplied dancers. His office was at the top of a dingy building in Soho. I was ushered in to see him (and this was not easy for he was so small his head hardly came above the top of the desk.) He had cunning eyes, slanting, Japanese style, and a lascivious mouth with very thick lips. His hands were clasped in front on the desk. He asked me to remove my coat and stand before him. His eyes narrowed as they took in my figure in its plain blue dress, and I shuddered as they travelled down from my head to my feet. A large tongue came out to wet his lips. Then, still looking at me he said:

"You're rather nice girlie. I like you, you got a bit o' class. Nice hair, your bust's alright and your waist. Now I'd like to look at your tops."

I was flustered, not knowing what he meant, too shy to ask. I noticed a seedy curtain at the far corner of the room. Had I brought a pair of shorts to slip into? I had not so he told me to go behind the curtain and put on a pair that hung on a hook. Hating it and feeling his eyes on my back, I squirmed my way to the curtain, thankful to disappear behind it, and with nervous fumbling hands, pulled on the shorts. Later I emerged, pink in the face in front of the curtain. The Japanese eyes gleamed for a second then they rested on my tops - his jargon for thighs.

"Pull yer skirt up girlie, right up - are yer shy? Now turn round slowly."

I felt like a chicken on a spit. Presently he called out to someone:

"Lil, can yer come 'ere a minute and take a look at this girl....might be alright for the Sugar Plum." In answer to the call a large, blousy, black haired woman emerged from a door at the side. She was smoking a cigarette and she gave me a quick practised look, one that an expert might give to a racehorse.

"Can you make an entrance on your points?" she asked me. Yes I could do that. They conferred together. Then:

"Take your shoes off" said the woman "and waltz round the room." It was hardly more than eight feet by six feet.

"Ter see how yer move" the man explained. "Just a few steps in front of me desk."

'Not with you' I thought, in wild panic, 'why you'd hardly come up to my bust!' I suppressed an awful desire to burst out laughing and bent to remove my shoes.

Two pairs of eyes followed me as I begun to cavort, gingerly around the tiny room.

"That'll do" said the woman after a few seconds. Again they conferred. Then came the verdict.

"Well girl, as I told yer, yer bust's alright and yer waist's fine, but the tops won't do - too plump for the fairy. Get them down and the part's yours, three months run at the Grand Theatre, Halifax, ten pounds a week."

As I came out into the afternoon sunlight I resolved to starve the tops down so that even Miss Leigh would be envious. But the road to hell....

All was not lost though, for while I did not achieve my goal, the lascivious agent seemed keen to engage me, and I became one of the dancers in the **Babes In The Wood** pantomime at Croydon. Once again I found myself working with Ralph Reader who was the producer. He was also playing 'Simple Simon' and had written most of the songs. He was a grand person to work for and the show was well produced and packed out each night. I had scruffy digs but I was happy. On my first morning I was wakened by a voice saying; "With or without sugar, ducks?" Turning round I saw a large bald head just level with the mattress, and holding a cup of tea.

I learned afterwards that one of the dwarfs from 'Snow-White' then running at a nearby theatre, was sharing my digs.

"Perfect little gentleman" said my landlady "Last week it was a giant from '**Jack And The Beanstalk**.'"

****

CHAPTER XV.

SINGING IN THE RAIN

As I tried to work out my future I thought of Leo, now working all out on his book. I would miss our Sundays together. Of course we would write to each other and he would probably want me to help with Shawn again. Would it best I wondered, to carry on with the present company until Christmas and then go home and sort out my career? I would need to live in London and perhaps take a refresher course in dancing.

I thought of my sister Felicity, now married with a little girl of six and a baby on the way. I knew I could always stay with her. She had a keen interest in the theatre from the days when we were Hollywood crazy and spent hours pasting photos of our idols into scrapbooks. A girl of many talents, she had made puppet dolls of Shirley Temple, Gary Cooper and Fred and Ginger. They bore an uncanny resemblance to the stars. She could also sketch well and model in clay. While on holiday she had been invited to join that seaside repertory company that I was in. For three weeks we had the fun of acting together. With her bright beauty and her quick mind she was an asset.

Yes, I could stay with Felicity, could help her when her baby came and her help to me would be invaluable. She always gave me the push I needed to go after agents, get photos taken; and she was so companionable, we shared the same sense of humour, a love of the absurd, and above all we had an affinity.

While most of his time was taken up with writing, Leo had let his appearance go hang. He had enough to do with the daily shopping, cooking his meals, seeing to the boats. He had to make do with washing just the collars and cuffs of his shirts, and giving a quick comb to his hair.

One afternoon he turned up at Harebell. I had no warning. We were all having tea. A spotless cloth, as usual, was on the table and the goodies spread out. Mrs. Bacon was the first to see him. She almost jumped out of her seat.

"Moi dear loife who's that?" I looked out and saw a face at the window.

"It's Leo" said Doreen. I felt acutely embarrassed, like a child when relatives arrive on sports day at school and talk in loud voices. I wanted to slink away for I sensed that Leo would not appeal to Mrs. Bacon. But the ball was in my court and she turned to me for an explanation:

"Oh that's my friend" I said, starting to get up.

"I'll go to the door" said gentle Percy, adding "A friend of yours is a friend of mine m'dear." Leo by this time was knocking on the window pane in a cheery way. He looked simply terrible; his hair was quite wild and he was wearing his most ancient jacket and faded denims. The old scruffy rucksack was on his back. I felt my toes curl. Then Percy brought him into the room and invited him to join us around the table. He took off the rucksack which was exuding a strong smell of fish, and plonked it down on to the floor. Then he smiled shyly at everyone, and I thought I saw his eyes light up when he met mine.

"My God, I had a hell of a journey on that bus" he began, "The damn thing went all the long way round." In those days it was rare to hear blasphemy round the teacups, especially in a bourgeois household. All eyes were on him except Doren's. She had subsided into helpless giggles and was spluttering into her tea. He put a hand on her shoulder. He must have guessed she was laughing at him but he understood. "How are you honey?" he said. Mrs. Bacon poured him some tea and passed the cakes to him. He took one gratefully.

"Yes, it's a damn awful ride" he went on "I had to take time off from my book to see the manager of Smiths. I knew you weren't far away" he added, to me.

Mrs. Bacon seldom took her eyes off his face. I think he was aware of her close scrutiny for he was talking more than he usually did. He asked her if she would like some fish, he had caught them pulling across the harbour. There was an awkward pause. She did not look over keen, but finally she decided to try a few.

"Are you coming to our play tonight?" Doreen asked.

"We're doing "**Hatter's Castle**" I told him, "I die coughing in the last act and she hangs herself. It's a jolly play." He laughed. "A gloomy devil Cronin, but a damn good writer." He couldn't come along because of leaving the boat too long at the Quay. It was a Spring tide that week.

Later as I walked with him to the bus stop he said "I just had to come and see you, I've been mising you like hell."

Seeing him out of his own setting gave me a different slant, and I tended to view him through the eyes of other people. I wondered what Mrs. Bacon would think of him. I was soon to know for I could not help overhearing her as I went back into the house.

"Looked as though he hadn't washed for a week....what do she see in him....I wouldn't have that article handed on a plate if it 'twas me....wouldn't have 'ee as a gift."

"Poor Leo" I said to Doreen later, "Picture him standing on a plate being handed to her."

"I'll never forget her face when she saw him; those awful old clothes he had on, I didn't know where to look."

I suddenly felt sad. I pictured him going back alone on the bus, then pulling across to the old hut. And he had come all this way to see me.

****

Christmas was approaching with its impending separation - Doreen to Liverpool - me to my home town. One rainy Sunday afternoon Leo and I went to see a marvellous film. It was called 'Singing in the Rain'. He had smartened up and was wearing his most becoming shirt and pullover. It was a showery trip in the boat coming back and we were getting nicely dry by the fire with me making toast.

"What a perfect film" said Leo "and what a perfect day. How I wish you didn't have to go back tonight....or any other night come to that."

I went on making toast, happily anticipating his next words.

"You know you've saved my life" he said " Do you know that? I don't know what I would have done all these months without you; as I said before, I would have cracked up completely."

It was strange I thought how often in my life I had been most happy when it was raining. I could hear it now pouring down on the corrugated roof. Presently Leo said:

"Stevey darling, you know what has happened don't you?" I turned to face him, he was sitting in his old comfortable chair. There was so much love in his eyes.

I forgot about the toast.

And then suddenly everything became clear to me as though a mist had lifted, and I was in his arms and he was holding me tight against him.

"I've been wanting to tell you this" he said "I thought....I hoped you knew. I love you Stevey....I love you so much."

I felt the quick sense of triumph every woman knows when she thinks she has made a conquest. But I was silent, happy to feel loved, to feel his arms around me. I think I knew then that we were going to make a life together.

Autumn Gold

Leo pulled the settee over to the fire. I don't know how long we sat there, putting off the moment when I would have to catch that bus back to Harebell. Choo-i was looking through the window from his perch on the balcony, a disdainful look that said 'silly humans, why bother with buses and timetables.'

"Oh to hell with the bus "said Leo "I'll see you catch the last one. I hate you living there anyway, for when you love someone they should be near you and, hey (he gave me a nudge) I still don't know if you feel the same, you never will tell me." By way of an answer I nestled even closer to him and gave him a hug.

"You know" he said, after a while "I'm a poor proposition for you - you'd better not tell your family what a financial jam I'm in at present! Dear oh dear, singing in the rain!"

"Yes, but you'll be better off when the book's finished, it should bring in some money."

"It won't be all plain sailing at first, I warn you, though no one has ever starved with me. But it will be a life. One day, you and I, we'll do great things together."

The wind was blowing now, quite hard, showing me that there can also be winter at Paradise Creek. We were silent for a while, listening to the rain, when Leo said;

"The world will be against it, and you at least will have to live in the world."

For a long time afterwards I pondered over those words.

We talked of many things. We talked of the future, and past joys like the holiday which now seemed so long ago.

"Do you remember our picnic at Lerryn?" said Leo "I'll never forget that day. Such colours, the setting sun.... and the river banks. I think it was then that I first fell in love with you Stevey, on the shores of Lerryn Creek.... with the blue smoke from the bonfire and your golden hair."

It was still raining hard when, much later we rowed out to *Amanda*. She was looking rather cross, bobbing about a lot on the water. I fancied she must have heard our talk. "She's very jealous today" said Leo, taking the covers off. Her engine started with an angry roar, startling the seagulls off the deck. Leo throttled her down, then did his usual drill of climbing on to the deck to cast off the anchor. Then with his face shining wet, but eyes bright as stars, he left the tiller for a second, and cupping his hands to his mouth called: "Will you marry me?

CHAPTER XVI.

STEPHANIE'S DILEMMA

I did not sleep that night. Too many thoughts were spinning around in my head. I thought of Leo's proposal as the rain had poured down and the engine chugged, of the film we had seen together with that sublime song running through it that would always haunt me.

'The world will be against it.' It was true. He was old enough to be my father, yet his looks belied this for he was slim and so active with the boats and gardening, and our long walks. No one could say I was marrying for money for he hardly had any. Like Mr. Micawber, he was always waiting for something to turn up, like a film offer for one of his books.

Still I could not sleep. I crept downstairs and made myself some coffee and then sat up in bed drinking it, and thinking. What would the family's reaction be?

One thing was certain. Before I met Leo his wife had made it clear that their marriage was over. She would never come back to him.

Did I really want a quiet life, as quiet as this would be up a Cornish creek? I who loved the social life, dances and parties, the theatre, loved fooling about in the repertory company and having nonsense jokes with Doreen?

I thought of Colin and his quite obvious charm. It would be goodbye to him. I had seen him once again before he went back for the Autumn term. I was not in love with him, but the friendship could have developed. Like me, he too enjoyed the lighter side of life.

Two days later there was a letter for me with the now familiar writing on the envelope.

"No I don't want an answer yet! Let me go on dreaming. I couldn't stand another knock at present, I need all my courage, all my illusions to finish the book." After giving an indication of how the future might be shaped, how he would like to see it shaped, the letter ended on a wistful note: "How I wish that you were here, and loved me".

I think I had already made up my mind to marry Leo. I knew that I would miss the stage: the world of make-believe was more appealing than the real one. I would miss a great many other things too. I knew that there would be friends that would advise against it, and that I too might have second thoughts. But I felt attached to him, could not see a future without him, and therefore I followed my heart.

When I told Doreen she did not believe me. She was so used to all the clowning and tomfoolery we went in for that she thought it was just another gag. When I did manage to convince her she became thoughtful and strangely serious. She urged me to think it over carefully, and pointed out all the disadvantages. At the same time she made it clear how much she liked Leo. I had long been impressed by her capacity for hard work and study and I now realised that she was both level headed and wise.

Mrs. Bacon let me know her opinion straight out:

"You'm proper soft somewhere Stephanie, that's all m'dear" she said.

Shortly before Christmas we were due to leave Harebell, sadly, for we had loved it there, and loved our digs. We were going to wind up with a pantomime, roping in the local talent, and there was much to do learning songs and sketches..

I hadn't replied to Leo's letter right away. I would have to snatch a quiet moment.

And so, while everyone was asleep that night, I sat up in bed and I wrote down all those things I found so difficult to say.

A letter came bounding back. "Hadn't dared open yours until I'd got back, washed up, lit the fire and made some tea. She's got a job, I thought, a six months contract. Colin's given her a diamond necklace and a gold watch, and he's booked first class to India. The family has had a conference. All have said 'We've just got to put the iron curtain across Cornwall'. She's got bronchitis, appendicitis, she's broken her leg! And then I read your letter, I really am too excited to write. I want to dance and sing; and climb up a tree and swim in the creek; and paint a huge abstract picture and write a play and dig up the garden and plant a million tulips...."

I don't know how many times I read those words. The joy in them, the wild exuberance raised my spirits and filled me with hope for the future.

With promises to write and visit whenever we could, we bade a sad farewell to Mrs. Bacon and Percy, and as we helped to heave the props and scenery into the van Doreen gave a sigh. "I wonder if we'll ever be so happy in digs again."

In that magical part of world anything can happen.

When we arrived at the next village, somewhat prettier than Harebell, we were in luck for this time there was no tramping from door to door.

Instinct drove Doreen and me towards a white gate, along a small path to a delightful, almost miniature cottage with a garden in front. An old lady with snow white hair answered the door. I was at once arrested by her face for it was one of such sweetness and purity that she seemed hardly to belong to this material world. She accepted us without question and did not want to take any money. At the mention of terms she flushed with embarrassment so we had to insist on it. Finally she suggested a contribution so small as to be merely a token, and then she bade us follow her into the cottage where there was a bright fire and all was spotlessly clean and smelling of polish. She called to her husband who was pottering outside and he came in and shook hands. He had the same white hair and an angelic face. As she began to tell him about us I think she must have thought, in her innocence, that we were orphans from a storm with nowhere to live.

"I couldn't have turned them away" she told him "These dear little girls."

"Am I dreaming?" I whispered to Doreen "For you just don't meet people like this in real life."

It was not like real life at all. It was just like the stories you read as a child from a favourite book. "And the the weary travellers suddenly came upon a beautiful little cottage...." Soon we were following the old lady upstairs and into a bedroom with two lovely high old fashioned beds, thick white eiderdowns, solid mahogany furniture and flower patterned wallpaper. I was reminded of Rupert Bear's bedroom in his house at 'Nutwood'. A small window, framed by pretty curtains, overlooked a garden that, in summer time, would be a mass of flowers.

From then on we were mothered, ministered to and plied with food so that each meal was a feast. "This is your home my darlings, for as long as you wish" we were told, and the kind husband nodding in agreement "You can live with us my dears."

A little cottage, without many of the modern amenities like a bathroom and inside loo, yet I have seldom seen such cleanliness, or met a pair who radiated so much happiness. We stayed there for four happy weeks while we presented our plays at the village hall. The locals were friendly and came along to support us.

Shortly before Christmas Tony called a meeting to say there would be a week's holiday and that he wished everyone a good time. Afterwards the tour of Cornwall would continue and he gave a date and place for the company to reassemble.

Autumn Gold

As for me, the curtain was coming down on one of the happiest, craziest episodes of my life. I felt a pang as we all packed up the props and scenery. The old couple in the cottage cried when the time came for us to leave.

It was goodbye all round now. Before leaving Cornwall I went to Fowey to say goodbye to Leo and give him his present. I did not like leaving him but I knew that it would not be for long. He had been to see about his divorce and soon there would be no more partings.

I arrived about one o'clock. Leo was already at the bus stop. He was very excited. A film company had come down. They were going to make a film in Fowey, starting after Christmas. He had been talking to some of the actors on the Town Quay, and we were invited for drinks.

There was a spring in Leo's step as he walked down the hill. Hope, never far below the surface, bubbled up in him again. Perhaps....who knows....his **Love in the Sun** would be made into a film! At last....at some future date, maybe....he might interest them. I felt happy too. I loved the company of actors as they had this warmth about them, rarely found in other people.

The town had a festive air about it. The shops were gaily lit and decorated and most of the houses had a lighted tree at the window with tinsel and silver balls. I loved to get a glimpse inside and see the paper chains and lanterns hanging from the ceilings, and the bright fires. Christmas was wonderful. If only we could all be together.

We were to meet our new friends at a certain pub near the Town Quay. They were already there, sitting at the bar when we arrived, about six of them. Introductions were quickly made, although I could have picked them out as film or theatre folk.

We were all enjoying ourselves and having a nice session until I chanced to get talking to one of the actors sitting next to me. He was not a star but one who had played supporting roles in several British films, mostly character parts. In the course of conversation I told him that Leo and I were getting married. After that it was like a scene changing, a dream going wrong. He reacted with fascinated horror.

"You're going to marry him?" he said "HIM? Why you must be mad....mad. You tell me, you're going to throw your life away, live up a backwater!"

"It's not just a backwater" I said, stung by his crudeness "it's a beautiful Cornish creek."

Luckily Leo had slipped away to see to the boat. The actor was staring at me in a pop-eyed sort of way. He was middle-aged and not at all attractive. I could tell that he had been drinking a lot for there was a strong smell of whisky and his face was a dull red. He lurched towards me.

"Don't do it lass" he said "You're young and lovely....don't give up the stage....come to London....I know all the right people....We'll have you a star in the West End."

Although gullible, I did not fall for this old line. He went burbling on about London and the various producers he could introduce me to, when Leo returned and the conversation came to a halt. I felt dreadfully embarrassed and tried to shake off the actor and talk to some of the others. Then Leo, perhaps scenting danger, said we really ought to be getting back. He had enjoyed talking to them all, and telling them about his film **Turn Of The Tide** which had been adapted from one of his books and was J. Arthur Rank's first big project.

The rest of the party had other plans. They wanted to prolong the session, get some drink and all go back to where they were staying. Leo would not be drawn in spite of much persuasion. The actor turned to me: "What about you coming? We can get you back later." I did not care about the drink, and certainly not about the actor, but I wanted very much to go to the party. The others grew more and more persuasive. We were all on the Quay with Leo about to bring the boat round to the steps. The actor kept urging me to go with them.

"Come along and enjoy yourself."

"You're only young once" said one of the others.

I went up to Leo who was untying the painter. "let's go" I said, " It would be fun....I know that man is pretty awful," I kept my voice down, "but we can soon lose him." But still Leo would not be drawn.

"You go if you like" he answered "but count me out. I was looking forward to our having lunch together, and then perhaps a trip up the river but,....well never mind." The actor cut in again.

"Oh come on, come and enjoy yourself. You don't want to get stuck up the creek!" I hesitated. His words in the pub had disturbed me. I felt shaken. Suddenly I had real doubts about giving up the stage. I felt that I was now at the cross roads, and there was this sign-post pointing — in one direction —life up the creek, — and the other — life on the stage.

Then Leo, with quiet dignity, took the painter and brought the boat alongside the steps. I could tell from his back view that he was hurt. He stepped into the boat and sat down. Then he asked "Are you coming with me?" He was already reaching for the oars. "No wait!" I cried, for he looked so sad, "I've decided, I'm going to come with you Leo."

****

It was sad saying goodbye to Doreen. Another of life's chapters had closed. Tears were streaming down her face as the train came in. She was catching the same one as Joe, to Liverpool. They got in and I talked to her through the window.

"I can't imagine being in digs without you" she said.

As I blew my nose and mopped my eyes I hoped very much that the future would hold something bright for her.

"Don't ever stop being silly and mad and making faces" I said.

"Or you" she sniffed " All my memories will be happy and funny ones."

"I wonder if we will ever laugh so much again?"

"Oh it's going to be horrid" cried Doreen, with a fresh burst of tears. Joe had come to stand next to her.

"Never mind," he said, "you'll have me."

Something in his look made me feel that everything was going to turn out alright for her.

****

Mother was excited to see me again, and eager to hear all about the tour and the new friends I had made. She had plenty to tell me herself, including a piece of information that left me dumbstruck. "Oh by the way, a telegram came for you" she said. "It was some time ago now, from Mary Hayley Bell, that's John Mills wife, she's a playwright. She wanted to see you about a small part in **Angel** a play she has written herself, that has come on in the West End. I didn't send it on for you seemed so happy down in Cornwall and it wasn't as though you had definitely landed the part."

I remembered meeting John Mills and his wife at the Noel Coward party. They had been so friendly and pleasant. So she must have remembered me.

I stared at my mother incredulously. I felt numb with disappointment. I reached for my coat and went outside, over the road and on to the beach. I stood there for a while watching the rough grey sea. And I thought how another of my golden chances had passed me by.

****

CHAPTER XVII.

SEA BOOTS FROM NOW ON

There was ample time to think things over before getting married as Leo did not get his divorce until two years later. In that time I could have attempted to join another repertory company. I certainly did not want to remain idle, but I was, as my landlady had pointed out, completely fascinated by Leo and I just wanted to be with him or at least, near him. So I filled in the waiting period by getting a job in one of the hotels in Fowey. It was part time, mostly laying tables and typing menus, but I had to be there early in the morning so Esme let me stay with her.

Leo collected me every afternoon, my free time, and we went across in his boat to the hut. He was working all out on his book **The Golden Waterwheel** and had a batch of pages ready for me to type. I was no expert, but a lot quicker than he was. It was also helpful for him to be able to read aloud to me the chapter he had written, and I could share his excitement in seeing the story take shape.

Shawn continued to come for the holidays and I managed to get time off to help Leo with him. Once Henrietta brought him down and on another occasion I had the pleasure of meeting Ann and Simon.

By the end of 1953 Leo had finished **The Golden Waterwheel** and had sent it off to Collins Publishers who had been allowing him a monthly sum in advance of royalties. Next came the arduous task of reading and correcting the proofs. I could not help with this for it was his book and only he could know if he wanted to make any alterations. Only when the proofs had been sent back could he relax for a while, weary, but satisfied that his job was done. "I feel like a mother who has produced a kid" he told me. "My book is my baby."

Early the following summer the first copies of the book arrived. It was quite thrilling to see them, about a dozen altogether, these were complementary copies. The jacket was attractively bright with a design of a yellow waterwheel in front of a red house surrounded by land and lush greenery.

During publication week Leo was keyed up and anxious. He bought all the Sunday newspapers, and together we read the reviews of the book, exclaiming over the good ones. The critics described it as a happy book, and Hatchards in Regent Street displayed several copies in their front window.

Leo took a break before starting work on **The Happy Ending**, his wartime story set in Wales. It was part of his contract to produce books at regular intervals, but being slow and meticulous it took him about two years to write one. He was always on the look out for new ideas. "One day you've got to have a shot at your book" he told me " and I'm going to keep nagging you about it for I know you can do it."

Leo could not promise that our life together would be all plain sailing - whose life ever is? But he was confident that we could make a go of it.

During the two years of my friendship with Leo there had been no real attempt by my family to intervene. Mother had come down to Cornwall and stayed in our digs at Harebell. She loved meeting the company and seeing the plays. Doreen and I took her to Fowey to meet Leo who had pulled across the harbour in the dinghy. He had come straight from working on *Amanda* and the fast ebbing tide prevented him from smartening up. He apologised for his rough attire but mother had only smiled, a little uncertainly.

That night after I had gone to bed she came into my room.

"Do you like him?" I asked her rather anxiously. She straightened my bed covers, as though searching around for something to say.

"Well darling, let's just say I don't dislike him." She bent down to kiss me and quietly left the room.

Sometime after I had left the repertory company, my parents came and stayed at the hotel where I was working. Leo took us across in *Amanda* to see the hut. My father was not enthusiastic. The isolation of the creek horrified him "Suppose anyone gets ill up there?" He did not share my mother's love of boats because he could not swim and the water scared him. But he agreed that Fowey was enchanting and enjoyed visiting the different pubs.

Leo knew that my parents were looking him over, that they would obviously want to have a heart to heart talk with him: It was their duty after all. So one evening my father took us all out to dinner at a riverside hotel. He ordered a bottle of wine. Leo looked nervous, my mother somewhat severe. Halfway through the meal my father cleared his throat - better to get the wretched thing over, and how he hated it.

"Leo" he began, for he too was nervous, "what exactly is going on between you and Steve?"

Leo loked at my parents and his face coloured. "I'm in love with her" he answered simply "I'm hoping we can get married once my divorce comes through." My father noticed that Leo's hand was shaking and offered to refill his glass. Then mother leaned forward.

"And how" she asked "do you propose to support her?"

There was a moment's silence. Then Leo threw out his arms.

"I'm an artist" he told her.

Luckily my parents knew better than anyone, that writers, like actors, live precariously by their talents and can seldom retire as their work does not afford them a pension. Then Leo told them about his last book and the royalties he had received, which though not high, had kept him afloat. He hoped to do better with his next one which he was working on. Finally he assured them that he had a strong sense of responsibility and no-one had ever starved with him.

By November 1954 Leo was granted a decri nisi. Soon he would be free to marry. By this time I had left my job at the hotel and was back living with my parents. It was a good time to go visiting my relatives.

One member of the family showed her disapproval of me in a thoroughly outspoken way. My aunt Daphne was now living in Grosvenor Street and carrying on with her exclusive lingerie business. When I called on her she was putting a tuck in one of her glamorous nightgowns. She knew all about my affairs and came straight to the point.

"I'm shocked and upset at what I've heard" she told me, crossly biting off a piece of thread "and as for your poor parents...." A long lecture followed.

"But they like Leo" I said, when I could get a word in.

"Liking is one thing, and I am sure he is a very nice man, but to tell us all that you're going to marry him, a man years older than you and live in a hut up a deserted lonely river! How do you expect your family to react to this?"

"They haven't actually said they disapprove."

"Perhaps they don't like to....you've always been indulged. When I think of all your mother has done for you," Daphne's eyes were heavy with reproach. "The lovely childhood you had, with all the treats and presents and fun.... poor mummie. How could you worry her like this?"

As I prepared to leave my aunt's flat I felt chastened. But I put my arms around her and gave her a kiss. I knew she had my interests at heart.

In search of reassurance I set off to visit my sister Felicity. She and her husband lived in Peckham, South London. Their second child had been born and another was on the way. Over cups of tea and a plate of her homemade ginger flapjacks we had a heart to heart talk. Felicity had met Leo during one of his rare visits to London. "She's as lovely as you described her to me" he said afterwards. I looked at the girl who had been my dearest friend and confidante since nursery days.

"Do you think I should marry him sister?" We often used this term of address, a throw-back to childhood games. She paused, about to dunk her buscuit, and looked away reflectively. Then:

"I think you might be very happy with him" she said "I liked him at once when I met him, and you've so much in common."

"But the difference in our ages, what do you think about that?"

"Well....obviously you won't grow old together, but in a world so full of broken marriages, if you have ten or fifteen years together it would be something to look back on."

She was smiling encouragingly at me, her little girl now perched on her lap, she looked radiant. I remembered how I had always admired her looks, the way her auburn hair fell in a lovely loose wave down one side, her large grey-blue eyes. And I remembered how devoted she had been to me when we were little, how she stuck up for me, especially at boarding school where she was often punished unfairly for things I did wrong. Coupled with all this, Felicity had strength of character and faced life with courage.

I came away from that happy home feeling more positive and confident about the future.

****

Just three months after Leo was granted the decree nisi, I took the plunge and we were married at St. Austell, Cornwall.

"BRIDE SAILS TO LONELIEST HONEYMOON." " HER HOME A LONELY CREEK." This was how the daily and provincial papers described it. One however was more dramatic:

"BRIDE BIDS FAREWELL TO FAMILY AND FRIENDS AND GOES TO LIVE ON THE SHORES OF ISOLATED BACK WATER." According to the press we had a 'luxury yacht' and went on a 'honeymoon cruise'. There had apparently been a big reception attended by many celebrities of the literary and show business world. The local newspapers went into more personal details with:

"AUTHOR MARRIES ACTRESS" and then went on to give our ages. "SEA BOOTS FROM NOW ON" might have been a more apt title. This was the summing up from one of the guests as she drank to our health at the reception.

It had been a quiet affair, our February wedding. Wilfred from the sailing club was best man. He presented us with flowers for the occasion, a spray of freesia for me and a carnation for Leo and himself to wear. My mother gave us a small reception which was held in a room above the Toll Bar Restaurant in Fowey. It was warm and intimate, just a few close friends and family. I was unable to have all the people that I wanted. Felicity was too far pregnant (with twins), my father could not make it owing to pressure of work and Daphne du Maurier was in Paris.

A high-light of the occasion which came as a wonderful surprise and had been inspired and organised by mother, was a most original cake made in the shape of one of Leo's novels. It was beautifully decorated with the title **Sally Lunn** iced on to the 'jacket'.

It seemed a shame to cut it.

****

CHAPTER XVIII.

THE SIMPLE LIFE.

Cold February and me in the kitchen, for I spent most of the mornings there while Leo took his mug of coffee into the front room, firmly shutting me in — "Must get on with the book honey." It was a quaint honeymoon, if you could call it such. Like Winnie The Pooh, nose pressed to the window pane, I looked out at the quiet scene.

'I'm a bride of one week' I thought, and drew a face on the steam of the window.

Slowly I adjust to isolation. The trees are bare....snow comes; so at last does Spring. Flowers appear on the high land, bluebells, pink campion, cuckoo pint and mimosa. Everything blooms out. We go to Lantic Bay for seagull eggs. Beautifully the Spring comes to Cornwall. Then early summer, with the honeysuckle, and the creek calm.

I soon found plenty to do while Leo was working. I smartened up the doors with fresh paint and made new curtains. I learned how to make stews and chocolate cake in the calor gas oven. When the weather was right I rowed across to Fowey and did the shopping and collected the milk and mail. On the way I sometimes put the line overboard and caught a pollack. In the afternoon we usually did something nice, a trip in the boat or calling on friends. A lot of people came to see us which was surprising as we were so isolated. They hired boats or came along the top path. Bob and Joyce sailed up in their own boat which Bob had built himself. There was jam making from blackcurrants that grew in abundance near the path. Later there would be blackberries to pick with the help of Shawn, my stepson now. They grew in the garden, on the land above and all the way up the path to the pink cottage.

I was happy. Shawn was coming that Easter, and again in the summer. I had already started swimming in May, and sun bathing on the lawn.

Sometimes when the mullet and bass were about we would wait until dusk and set the net. Then I would row very gently round the creek while Leo began paying out the net bit by bit. He kept a watch on it by going several times down to the water. Keeping my clothes on I would go to bed for a while and be woken up at three in the morning. It was nice and unusual to get up at that hour and we would hurry down to haul in the net.

There was great excitement in finding a large bass or two, and once there was a salmon trout.

There was an abundance of free food up the creek. As well as prawns there were mussels, winkles, cockles and oysters. The vegetables in the garden were enriched by the seaweed that Leo carried up in sackfuls from the cove. He grew spinach, cabbages, peas broccoli and scarlet runners (his pride). The fruit trees he had himself planted yielded apples, plums and pears.

Apart from the age difference it was a good match. We shared a love of natural beauty, the countryside, music, art and the theatre, and mostly we enjoyed the same books.

Our faults were similar too. We did not really like being untidy, and longed to create an orderly effect. While I often achieved it and had rows of cups hanging neatly on their hooks and a well wiped table, I could not somehow keep it up. I never knew why or how there came to be marmite on the mantlepiece or nylons in the knife drawer.

Around the end of July I developed a strange aversion to marmalade and a craving for crisps. I woke feeling decidedly odd and could not face any meals except tomatoes on toast. Was this morning sickness? A baby on the way. A baby! I felt a sudden rush of joy.

Because I lived very much in a world of my own, I had never really thought about becoming a mother. Somewhere at the back of my mind I knew that I wanted a child and that I would regard one as the most precious of life's gifts. Always susceptible to the charm and pathos of children, I viewed them sometimes with awe. They were so perfect, so new, that I believed in Wordsworth's theory, they come trailing clouds of glory. You had only to look at their rounded arms and legs, see the soft curve and bloom on their cheeks to realise they were often superior to adults in physical beauty.

By August my suspicions were confirmed. I was very happy and excited and also a bit scared. I had heard many frightening things about childbirth and the risk of complications. The very word labour had a grim significance. Women had described their 'ordeal' to me in detail. "I lay groaning for hours in the most dreadful pain." "If the doctor hadn't come when he did...."

Leo was happy too, and a little bit jolted. "I'll have to work harder than ever on the book" he said "and try and make some money."

"I trust you're not thinking of having it over there" said the doctor. I wasn't. I knew that if things started to happen and *Amanda* was in one of her moods, I might be in a tight spot.

Changes would have to be made. The most important was to have electricity. Shawn said he could do it. He wanted to fix it all himself. We thanked him very much for his offer but explained that it would be best to leave it to Bob.

Before the end of the year we were all electric. Bob had made a brilliant job of it. It was goodbye now to the swaying Tilly lamps, and the small Aladdin ones that hung over the beds.

The baby was due the following April, on the 27th. As the months went by I felt nice and broody, it was a special sort of bliss preparing for the big event. The nursery would be at the far end of the hut near Shawn's room. I painted the chest of drawers, light blue-grey with orange knobs. I had matching curtains and Leo built a nursing chair and table to go beside it.

Friends and relatives sent baby clothes which they had made or knitted, tiny nightgowns, woolly vests and bootees. It was exciting when the gifts started arriving. From mother there was a high chair and a big soft shawl, and my aunts came up with a baby bath and basket.

I went for long walks in the morning and rested after lunch. During these solitary walks I pictured what it must be like to have a little figure beside me, holding my hand, calling me mummie. The actual birth seemed remote. I could not believe it would ever really happen. I could not see beyond it. It was like a vast mountain that I had to climb. Would I ever be able to get beyond it and down the other side?

My first Christmas at the hut. I put up decorations and prepared for Bob and Joyce who were coming to spend it with us. We got the big front room warm with both fires going, and Leo rowed across in the dinghy to fetch them, fishing all the way. *Amanda* was out of action due to the damp cold weather and her engine which was croaking a bit. She had to be kept warm and covered up. I felt rather sorry for her.

By the following March we had a telephone installed. We were getting quite mod. con. Only a month to go now before the big event.

It was April. I was having one of those periodic check-ups. My baby was due in a week's time. The specialist however had other ideas.

"The baby's getting too big" he told me "I think you'd better come into hospital at the weekend and we'll start things going."

"But it isn't due until the 27th" I reminded him. He waved that aside almost gaily.

"Oh, we'll have it born before then. You come into hospital on Friday and we'll get cracking."

It was a curious expression to use. What did he mean by 'start things going?' I hadn't the nerve to ask him.

However I soon found out.

I do not think any schoolgirl, starting her first term, could have been more scared than I was when I set off for the station. We each had a corner seat on the train. Leo looked out of the window, watching with a keen interest everything that went by. He never lolled on trains or stared vacantly.

I could think only of the one great adventure that lay ahead of me.

When we arrived at the maternity hospital I felt the same sick terror I used to have as a child when I had gas at the dentist. A nurse bustled forward,plump and capable, and showed us into a room with two beds in it. One was occupied by a lady who had a bright pleasant face. She smiled cheerfully at me. I returned it with a feeble one.

Leo could not stay too long because of the boat and tides. He lifted my case on to the bed. I felt I was going to cry. I did not want him to go. We talked for a little while, then the bustling nurse came in and asked me to unpack my things and get into bed. I walked down the corridor with Leo. Perhaps this would be the last time I would ever see him...."You'll be alright honey" he said, kissing me goodbye at the entrance door. "I'll phone tomorrow. I just know you've got the courage."

Back in the room I started to unpack. Then suddenly I could not help it, I burst into tears.

The following morning I was awakened by a very bright light glaring into my eyes, and an equally bright voice. "Good morning dear, did you sleep well?" Before I could answer a thermometer was thrust into my mouth. I mumbled something.

"That's right dear" said the night sister. She picked up my wrist and looked at her watch. I looked at it too. Although it was upside down to me I could see it was exactly five o'clock. I could hear a chorus of wailing and caterwauling coming from what must be the nursery at the end of the corridor.

'Wah wah wah...' and there was constant clanging and clattering going on in the sluice room opposite mine.

"Yes, we start the day early here" said the sister reading my thoughts.

"Now just turn on your side a minute, I'm going to give you an injection."

I watched as she filled the syringe, waiting to feel the sharp prick of the needle in my thigh.

"There!" She rubbed the place with a piece of cotton wool soaked in spirit. "We've got to get seven more of these into you before eleven. Your next will be in a quarter of an hour so just you remind those nurses if they forget." She went briskly to the door and added, "No breakfast for you, you'll be having a general anaesthetic later on." Before I could ask why, she vanished.

It was the cleaner who put me wise. Mopping around my bed and locker she told me darkly, "They're going to rupture your membranes. Doctor's coming along to do it soon."

Whatever went on while I was out cold, I do not know, but the baby refused to be disturbed, and all the other methods used to start things going didn't work either. After that I was left alone for a bit. Mothers came into hospital, had their babies and left before I had even started. The lady sharing my room had gone home with her baby before I had even a twinge.

Mothers were being admitted at all hours. My room was almost opposite the labour room. Sometimes when the door was opened I could hear moaning and groans, sometimes shrieks.

As time went on I began to feel like a permanent lodger.

I had no fear of going into labour now, only a great longing for the whole thing to start.

The 27th came and went without any stirrings from within. The following week it was decided that something must be done, so I was not allowed to be left in peace anymore.

It was Sunday, the sixth of May. There had been a second attempt to start things off, and by lunch time it had begun to work.

Certain things are clear to me that happened during the rest of the day, but like a dream much of it has faded. I was told to keep moving so I walked up and down the corridor rubbing my back. By the afternoon of the following day I was not allowed to walk. The pain was strong but I stayed on top and still thought what a great adventure it was.

I was now in the labour room on a high bed, wearing a hospital nightgown. On the wall opposite was a large cupboard with a glass front. I could see instruments of all shapes and sizes. By the wall at the head of my bed were stands with gas cylinders and beside me a table with a glass and a jug of water. In a small annexe to the room I saw sterilizers and drums.

Autumn Gold

Mr. Gordon, the specialist, had been to see me, and later that evening a sister tutor who gave lectures on midwifery came. She made me sit on a chair drawn up to the bed with my arms stretched out across it and my head between them.

I was in this forlorn attitude when the night sister came in to tell me Leo had just phoned.

"He sends you his dearest love" she said "and he's thinking of you every minute. Isn't that nice?" I did not answer just then. I was caught up in a wave of pain. Then slowly it died down again.

"Yes, thank you" I said.

The message moved me. A tear rolled down my face.

Shortly after this I was helped back to bed.

It was night time now. The cot was made up ready at the foot of my bed. The sight of it there was overwhelmingly dramatic and wonderful. I felt I was taking part in some great Olympic race and this was my goal. Now I was spurred on to greater endeavour. I would use all my strength to get this baby born.

The night sister came in again. She was carrying two hot water bottles. She put them in the cot between the blankets and gave me a meaningful look. I felt another pain.

Strange things had begun to happen, great forces taking charge. I was swept along by a powerful current and I knew instinctively that I must not resist. 'I shall be OK.' I told myself. Babies are born every minute.'

The sister and the staff nurse were with me. Labour was a very apt name I thought, hard labour.

"I hope you are going to have this baby after all" said the sister "and that we won't be going on like this all night and all tomorrow. You're very slow. What are we going to do with you?"

I wasn't conscious of any pain, but a series of urgent warnings. My efforts were similar to those of a man trying to launch a heavy boat that had grounded in the mud. The difference was in time. The man would have got his boat off long ago, he would not have gone on heaving indefinitely And could I? I could feel my heart pounding. At last the sister was pleased. She said I was doing well. "It won't be very long now" she told me.

I knew that the sister, an experienced midwife, was delivering babies at all hours, but the care and attention she was giving me made me feel special.

I was very thirsty and just about to ask if I could have some water when

The Simple Life

I saw Mr. Gordon and Dr. Evans, the anaesthetist, walk briskly into the room.

"Well' here we are again" said Dr. Evans, smiling and smoothing his hands together. "This is the culmination of a long nine months. You've been very good. We're going to give you a rest now. And when you wake up...." He went over to the trolley and paused a second. "When you wake up...."

Here Mr. Gordon cut in. "Yes, you've been very good and patient. Ah well. it won't be long now, will it sister?" He turned to her and she helped him into his green gown.

This was surely the most dramatic moment in my life, and all I could find to say was; "I do hope I haven't got you up for nothing!"

Mr. Gordon laughed heartily.

"What time is it?" I asked him. He looked at his watch.

"I make it just on four, four a.m."

Dr. Evans wheeled the trolley towards me.

"This isn't such a pleasant anaesthetic" he explained "but it's better for the baby." I felt I had no real need to be put out, but I imagined it was necessary.

Someone was pushing the bed into the centre of the room so that I was right underneath the big light. The pillows were taken away from under my head.

"Your religion dear?" asked the sister, her pen poised over a slip of paper. I did not really know what I was right then so I borrowed from Leo. "I'm a human atheist" I said, meaning humanist.

"I want you to take your time over this" said a voice behind my head. Something that resembled a dog's muzzle hovered over my nose and mouth.

"Please, could I have a drink of water first, I'm so thirsty."

"I'm afraid not dear, it wouldn't be good for you."

The muzzle hovered again.

"Hold my hand" I asked the nurse at my side. Instantly her hand shot out to me, firm and friendly; my last touch with the conscious world.

Straps were going around my face, over and over, like bandaging a limb. Only my eyes seemed to be free.

Then it came. I felt the full impact of it in my first hesitant breath. Savagely strong, hideously sweet, sharp, suffocating, choking fumes. A quick thought flashed through my mind 'I'll either wake up afterwards or I won't; and if I don't I'll be 'out' forever and ever and ever....'

Autumn Gold

Through a black fog, at the end of a long black tunnel I heard voices:

"Take your time my dear....there's no hurry....that's right.....deep breaths...."

"Forceps sister....thank you....and short blades."

More voices from the tunnel. They grew louder and louder. They became a whole chorus of voices chanting:

"Forceps....forceps...FORCEPS....FORCEPS!"

****

"Wake up dear! It's all over. Come on! Wake up.... You've got a little daughter....Come on....have a look at her. She's lovely."

Only two words registered on my heavily doped mind "daughter" and "lovely."

I struggled to come to from the deep anaesthetic. I was like a diver groping my way to the surface.

"Come on! Open your eyes. Look! We've something to show you!"

I opened my eyes, and turned my head to the direction of the voices.

I saw my baby. She was held proudly in the sister's arms, wrapped in a blanket. She wasn't red faced. She wasn't wrinkled or bald. She wasn't even crying. I saw every detail of her head and face. Her fair hair, her brow and temple; her eyes which were looking upwards, her nose, cheeks, mouth and chin. Everything about her seemed just right. She was perfect, I thought. She was all I could wish for.

My eyes filled with tears. I loved her.

I went on looking at her and loving her. I was too happy to speak.

****

CHAPTER XIX.

LIFE WITH OUR BABY

Life could never be the same again, nor would I want it to be. I was totally committed. The baby was my world.

Much has been written about mother love, but I never realised it would be so intense, so primitive. It changed me, I hope, for the better. From then on I grew up a little. I took more interest in world affairs, partly I suppose because I now had a very real responsibility. I wanted suddenly to clean and tidy up the world, to sweep up all the sadness, the ugliness and have it perfect.

She was born with a riotous sense of humour; often she would lie laughing in her cot and I would be woken up by the sound of happy chuckles. She was so beautiful.

I told everyone: "I have a baby that looks like Marilyn Monroe." Near silver blonde hair, dimples and a full mouth. Her eyes were large, framed by dark lashes. She was serene, content, as though the magic beauty of the place had flowed into her. Sometimes as I held her in my arms, felt her head nestling against me and saw the gentle look in her sleepy green eyes, I knew why I had named her Selina. In those moments I came as close to heaven as I will ever be.

Coming into the Autumn of Leo's life, Selina was a joy, a wonder to him. She gave him more happiness than he had known for years. He now had a child that was really his, not just lent out for holidays, and he showed his love in very practical ways. Ever watchful for her safety he set about making fireguards, protective netting against the nursery window. He made a soft canvas bath and a carry cot with nautical handles of rope so that we could take her with us in the boat.

In fine weather Selina was in the fresh air much of the time and was sun tanned all over. She had a firm body with no excess fat. She had her naughty moments, like all babies; sometimes rebelling against having her wispy hair combed or a woolly put on, she would trot away with me in pursuit, to find Leo.

Like all fathers when their young go to them for protection, he would be delighted, pick her up at once and say, "Ah, what is it baby? What's the matter? Had the old Goose been mean to you?"

Quickly she would catch on, "Ol' Goose, Ol' Goose!" and look at me over his shoulder.

"Come," he would say, "We'll go down to the cove and leave the old Goose." But her little arm would reach out to me, loyal.

I needed no baby book to do the fundamental things like changing and bathing her. Like the song, I did what came naturally, and fed her from my own supply.

Sometimes the baby would watch me intently from her cot as I busied about the nursery, dusting, folding away small garments. Leo loved to interpret her thoughts.

"Hurry up old Goose" he would say, pretending it was <u>her</u> talking, "I want my lunch."

"Alright baby" I would answer "it won't be long."

"Remember your job is looking after me."

"Yes of course baby."

"So get cracking Goose."

"Yes baby."

She seldom cried, but when she did, Leo just had to pick her up. As soon as he saw her pucker her mouth like babies do, and jerk her arms and legs imploringly, he would let down the side of the cot. "Do you think we should?" I would say, wondering if too much attention was bad, but he could not resist her.

In those early days, Selina and I were so dependent on Leo that we could not move from the creek without him. I could never have mastered the mysteries of *Amanda's* engine, nor could I row across to Fowey without his help in lifting out the carry cot. Obviously we couldn't have a pram, but later on we managed a push chair.

Partly because of being so isolated, I was forever anxious for the child's health and safety. I tried to shut out of my mind the awful thought of anything happening to Leo. If he was late coming back from a fishing trip I would stand by the window waiting anxiously for the first glimpse of *Amanda*. Fearful thoughts would cross my mind. Suppose he is out at sea and the engine has failed. Suppose he has fallen overboard while climbing on to the deck, had a heart attack - a stroke - he was just the age for it.

During these moments terror would grip me. I would leave the window and hurry back to look at our sleeping baby, lying there sucking the two middle fingers of her right hand, content, and yet so vulnerable.

"Oh baby, darling, how could I fend for you by myself? What will become of us?" Then back I would go to the window, watching, listening, or down to the water, just like Leo used to when he waited for me to return from a dance, and patrolled the cove with his lantern, like the biblical figure. What a dizzy relief it was to hear the faint chug, chug, and see the blue hull of *Amanda* coming into view, her porthole eyes looking fiendish.

Meanwhile nothing could spoil the joy and happiness that Selina gave us during those idyllic years. Although remote, it was a wonderful place to bring up a baby, quiet and peaceful, surrounded with natural beauty and with the purest air to breathe. We were both completely wrapped up in her. If this was wrong then we had no idea of it. We just loved her.

In the first few months I knew the sweet fulfilment of caring for someone small and helpless who needs you so much.

Leo was also having more happiness than he had known for years. This was the period he called his second life.

And Selina? What did she make of all this doting, adoring and anxious fussing? I think it would have been something like this:

From her cot the baby surveys her parents with her incredibly green eyes. She sees it all. She knows.... She has problem parents. Someday when she's a bit bigger she'll be able to cope with them, but right now she's landed — and there is no companion baby to discuss them with. Shawn is too big now. But she has Choo-i to confide in. Which of them is worst Choo-i? Purring softly, clawing at the carpet, he tells her, turning his amber eyes in my direction "You've got a heller there Selina."

One day, driven to despair by the quacking, flapping Goose who worries about everything, baby decides she must have a break. Unseen by the Goose, she trots down to the cove and makes her way purposefully to the jutting headland which she proceeds to climb over. She is travelling to Brazen Island, hoping perhaps for the company of other babies with similar problems.

But the Goose, washing small vests and rompers in the kitchen, gets a telepathic message 'The baby....she's gone very quiet!'....A quick look in the nursery....where is she?... panic stations, baby vanished! Goose tears down to the cove in time to see her baby turn sharp left and scramble over rocks. BABY!

"Selina! Come back!" Agonized Goose in hot pursuit of the tiny figure who now thinks a lovely game has started. Chuckling with fat laughter she speeds up a bit until she is trotting merrily towards the island. Frantic Goose bears down and sweeps up her young with one arm and carries her back to the hut. Quack, quack, quack! The baby, crushed at being thwarted, whimpers a bit at first, then, with a sigh, resigns herself to neurotic mother and plans to tell Choo-i all about it.

****

Shawn continued to visit us for the holidays and did not seem to mind having to share our attention with his infant sister.

He was quite pleased when she won second prize at the beautiful baby competition at the hospital fete.

****

CHAPTER XX.

SELINA

The porthole window on the door of Selina's nursery was convenient for having a peep through without disturbing her if she was sleeping. One morning after her bath, I was feeding her and I sensed that we were not quite alone. I looked towards the door and I saw two large eyes watching us through the porthole. Poor Shawn felt a bit left out.

Choo-i had to be discouraged from going into that room, but as time went on he and Selina became better acquainted. She was fascinated by him and by the marine life that was to be found on the shore. Once I heard peals of laughter coming from the nursery. I looked in and saw Selina, then about a year old, standing up in her cot watching Choo-i through the window. He was cavorting about in the oddest way, chasing his tail and sometimes spinning round in rapid circles. She was quite hysterical at the sight, holding on to the bars of her cot, doubled up with laughter.

In those early years Selina didn't see many other children. As time went on I began to have thoughts about a second one. She was far from being under privileged; she had toys enough to keep her happy and Leo had built her a doll's house, a rocking sea-horse and a swing at the end of the garden. Whenever possible he took her in the boat and sometimes carried her on his back up the spiral path towards Polruan. However, several of my friends were now expecting their second child and I began to get broody.

Then I realised with regret, that with our precarious life it would not be wise.

For a couple living in such an isolated spot we had a surprising number of visitors. They came on foot through the hills or by boat.

Voices carry on the water and often when I was down at the cove watching Selina at play, the pleasure boats went by on their way to Pont. Above the noise of the engine I could hear the boatman telling his cargo of passengers: "Leo Walmsley do live up there in that hut, and that's his young wife and baby daughter." We could also be seen by people on the opposite side of the creek as they walked through the hills.

Selina was a water baby. I taught her to swim at an early age and by the time she was three she was pulling that heavy boat.

Autumn Gold

Mother came to stay with us each May for Selina's birthday and sometimes she also came in the Autumn.. She loved the life we lived and thought
it all such fun, so quaint. A great lover of parties and the company of the
young, she was in her element decorating the birthday cake and the table,
organising games and decking her grandchild out in garlands of flowers.
She was enchanted to see the children arriving by boat, to hear their young
voices across the river as they called out, waving their gifts.

"What a thrilling way to arrive" she said " instead of catching silly
buses."

She loved boats, the fishing trips, and took it all in her stride. It was a
good job she had a sense of humour, and only laughed when she went to
have a bath and found a tin of wriggling worms in it.

Selina loved her visits. From the time she became mobile she hurried
along to her grandmother's room in the mornings, and climbed into her bed
for games and stories. They were great friends. Here was someone to confide in and to share secrets and whisper her longing for a pet of her own.
"Something that's alive and warm, that I can pick up in my arms and love."

Consequently all forms of marine life found their way to the nursery:
periwinkles, starfish, crabs.... She became devoted to a certain crab. He
was kept in a tank with stones and sea-weed. You do not get much response
from a crab, although Selina thought you did.

"Does crab love me?" she asked my mother, who assured her that the
creature did. Soon it was placed lovingly on a table beside her cot, and my
mother, going in to say goodnight, was asked to 'Kiss crab.'

Before long crab was taken out of his watery home to share the warmth
of the cot with his affectionate owner. Next morning a cold stiff creature
was found on the pillow beside her.

Apart from my mother we seldom had people to stay. The upheaval
would have caused disruption to Leo's writing. However, one year I managed to persuade him to agree to a visit from Myra, my Godmother, who
was also my aunt. She was a widow, childless, and lived alone in a rather
bleak area just out of London. I thought it would be a delightful break for
her to come for a few days.

It was Easter, very warm, and one of the nicest times to visit Cornwall,
with the Spring flowers now appearing on the high land.

Shawn's visit had been cancelled owing to an outbreak of chicken pox
at his school.

Selina

I set off in the dinghy with Selina who was now nearly three years old. *Amanda* was temporarily out of action having been brought ashore for minor repairs, but we didn't need her as the creek was dead calm. Myra was coming on a fast train to Par station. From there she would take the bus to Fowey.

"Are you going to pull the boat, baby?" Leo asked her.

He had come down to the cove and was coiling in the long rope from the trip anchor, while I kept an eye on Selina in case she went into the water in her new sandals. She was wearing a smart blue frock with a pattern of ships and stars. Her light golden hair shone like the sun and she smiled mischievously at him, hugging a large doll under one arm.

"You're not going to take that awful thing are you?" he said. H e h a d contempt for this doll which had been given to her by a kind relative. Stiff and angular, it was a gaudy looking thing with a painted face and eyes that stared straight ahead with a fixed expression. Mother for some reason had christened it 'Nora Docker' but Selina was quite fond of it.

"She wants to take her" I said.

"Want Nora Docker" said Selina, tightening her grip on the creature and sucking her middle fingers.

We lifted her into the boat and put her amidships where she sat looking small while I arranged the oars. "You give Nora to me" I said, stepping in "so that you can row." They were big oars for her to grasp but she managed.

Leo gave us a push off. He was full of paternal pride...."That's it, pull hard....my word, you are doing well."

A boat beneath a sunny sky. That was the poem that had come to my mind when I had first rowed up that creek. Watching Selina at the oars I thought of it again:

> *All in the golden afternoon*
> *Full leisurely we glide*
> *For both our oars with little skill*
> *by little arms are plied*
> *While little hands make vain pretence*
> *Our wanderings to guide.*

But this child did not lack skill, she put all she'd got into it with firm robust strokes, and we went quite a way almost to the mouth of the creek, when she'd had enough. We changed places and she set about hastily strip

163

ping Nora Docker's clothes off, right down to the buff, even to her gaudy necklace and bracelets.

As I pulled across the harbour I wondered if I had been wise to invite Myra. The fact that she was Catholic would not endear her to Leo who would be sure to challenge her about her faith. And she would most likely disapprove of our way of life.

I grew more despondent as we got nearer to Fowey. I wondered whether to give Selina a few hints on social etiquette or was it best not to bother one so young, almost a baby? I didn't want to teach her to say false things...and yet.... Better to leave it. Anyway, for the moment she was quite engrossed in washing Nora's bottom with a piece of wet seaweed.

"We're nearly there now" I said brightly. "Soon we'll be going up the big hill to see if auntie has arrived. She's coming on a green bus."

Young children seldom answer you straight away and when they do it can be disconcerting. However, Selina was too busy at the moment to make any comment. Then presently, in her low voice she said,

"Nora doesn't like her. She's just told me."

This was ominous Experience had told me that Nora's tastes and Selina's were strangely similar.

"Well that's a bit naughty of Nora because auntie is a very nice lady." There was a pause, but Selina could offer no explanation for Nora's attitude.

"She doesn't like her" she repeated firmly.

The tide was flowing now, gently lapping against the first step of the Albert Quay where two little boys stood fishing. I was careful to avoid their lines as we came alongside. A few people were leaning over the railings. One, whom I recognised as a local, called out;

"Throw me up the painter m'dear and I'll make fast for 'ee while you see to the little maid." Having done so, he came down, alongside the boat and lifted Selina out. As he set her down he took a step back and surveyed her with approval.

"She's 'andsome that one, growing away lovely. You got a smile for me then, my sweetheart?" He wondered, would I take her in to see his missus one day? For she was some troubled by arthritis and wasn't able to get about much. She would dearly love to see the maid.

Everyone was so friendly.

On our walk through the town we were hailed by more friendly locals who had a special greeting for Selina.

Selina

"Hello my lover! Hello my bird. Going shopping with mummie? Do those fingers taste nice?"

Some wanted to give her sweets, or biscuits. And the local 'bobby' on his beat hailed me "Lo Steve! Alright then?"

It was a long walk up the hill to the bus. It reminded me of when I was pregnant, how I had pictured the coming event as a great mountain to be climbed. Only I could not see beyond it, or ever believe I would arrive safely over the top. I remembered how I used to wonder what it must feel like to have a little child walking at my side.

With Selina's hand in mine, her other clutching Nora by the ankle, we went at a slow steady pace. I realised then that I had no regrets at leaving the stage. I now had something infinitely more dear to me than fame or fortune. And a voice that day seemed to say to me 'make the most of these years, they won't come round again.'

Myra had not been with us more than ten minutes when I began to have misgivings. She arrived with a grieved air complaining that the train was packed, she "couldn't get a decent cup of tea." I looked at her and wondered. She was tall with a rather high colour and eyes that snapped everything up, quick as a Hoover. She was wearing ridiculous clothes for stepping in a boat, high heeled shoes and a voluminous skirt which she drew together rather imperiously before seating herself astern. I just had time to wipe the seat made damp from Nora's toilet.

Pulling across the harbour I drew her attention to the charm of the water scene, the boats of various size, the colours. While she admitted it was very charming, she looked vaguely depressed when I suggested she might like to try for a fish.

"Me want to fish" said Selina, ready for anything. Leo had already baited the hook before we had left and there was a tin of fresh worms on board. She payed out her line and I pulled gently in case there were any pollack about.

As we approached the cove the sound of loud banging could be heard. I rounded the bluff and almost at once Selina cried:

"Look! Daddy on the floor!" and she chuckled. I brought the boat to a crunching halt and shipped the oars. Turning round I saw Leo lying flat on his back hammering away at the base of *Amanda*'s spine.

"Daddy!" cried Selina. He didn't hear her through the noise. I lifted her out - she had a little pair of red wellington boots on - and she hurried towards her father. Presently he got up and came over. He had put on an ancient pair of dungarees which were heavily stained with tar and paint.

"Sorry about this" he said, greeting Myra pleasantly, "but I've detected a slight leak in our boat and I'm fixing her with a piece of copper; she'll be seaworthy again after, but she's not safe at present."

My aunt glanced nervously at *Amanda* who was looking smug and pleased with herself.

"Stay where you are a minute" said Leo, noting Myra's absurd shoes. He selected some large, flat stones and positioned them as a landing stage. He then escorted her out of the boat, on to the stones, until she had safely embarked for the shore. "I'll join you presently" he said as we walked along, "but I want to get this job done before the tide comes up."

Myra took in Leo's appearance in one glance, then turned her attention to Selina who had settled herself down on the cove beside *Amanda* with a huge bunch of seaweed.

"Aren't you coming up with us?" Myra asked her, stooping down and opening wide her eyes like people do when addressing the very young. Selina regarded her thoughtfully. It was much more fun playing with the seaweed. If you pressed the pods they made a delightful popping sound.

Presently Myra straightened herself and went along towards the steps. I squatted down beside my daughter. "Come on Selina. Let's go up and show auntie where we live. She's going to sleep in that little room next to yours - won't that be nice?" Selina shook her head. Clearly I was on my own. Then as if to confirm this, I was given a sudden intimation.

"I'm not going to show her where the lavatory is."

Well,well. Thank you Selina. And thank you *Amanda*, for artfully spring-ing a leak. I looked daggers at the pair of them and *Amanda* stared at me through her porthole eyes. "I'll do your rudder a mischief next time" I told her.

It was going to be uphill work entertaining auntie, even Nora Docker didn't want to know.

The brightest thing was the weather. It remained consistently warm; but even this brought its problems, in the form of strange black flies. A swarm of them appeared in great profusion all over the garden. At first we thought that they were some kind of horse-fly, only they didn't sting. I was furious with them for arriving at the same time as our visitor: large ugly creatures, spoiling the pure country air. It was like a scene out of the film 'African Queen'.

There was nothing we could do about it. All bad things come to an end.

Selina

Easter Sunday looked like being the warmest day of all. The sun was shining brightly while I was getting the breakfast. Auntie had woken in a huff....No one knew why. She went into the garden to see if the black flies were still about. They were.

"Swarms of them all over the place," she said disgustedly "We won't be able to sit in the garden at all." She gave a deep sigh.

"I am sorry. We've never had them here before."

My aunt set about helping me to lay the table.

"Don't you find it lonely here sometimes, during the dark months?"

"No not really, it's rather snug. You've no idea how lovely it is in Autumn, how beautifully the bracken turns to gold. I go down to the water in the early morning. The air is crisp and sparkling and the mist is just rising from the creek. I stand and marvel at it, it's so peaceful and serene. I think how lucky I am to live here."

"Yes, we know it's a very pretty spot, but young company, I mean, don't you miss it?" I laughed. "I've got all the young company I need for the present." Again she sighed.

"Well, I don't know. It seems to me to be a very strange way to live: Hiding yourself away like this. Do you think of the future? Life must be faced."

'The world will be against it, and you at least will have to live in the world'. I thought of Leo's words that day.

Presently Myra asked, "Is Selina up?"

"Not yet. She's just had her Easter egg. Oh, you should have seen her little face when she opened the parcel!" I gazed out of the window for a second, "They're such darlings at this age, aren't they?"

"Watch it! You're burning the toast!" cried Myra and she added, "You mothers" and went off to see Selina. Seconds later she called out,

"You want to see her 'dear little face' now. I never saw such a sight." I hurried to have a look. Selina was sitting up in her cot munching blissfully. Chocolate was smeared all over her face and some had reached her hair. "I didn't know it" she said, looking up guiltily. "I'm only a little joke."

But auntie did not think so. "Fancy giving a child chocolate before breakfast!" she snapped.

"It's only once in a while. She seldom has many sweets. In fact I'm quite strict...."

"You had better let me wash her as you are getting the breakfast."

She lifted Selina down from her cot and took her to the bathroom. Then she dressed her in a clean cotton frock and white cardigan.

"That won't stay white for long," I thought.

"Has she a pinafore?" auntie enquired.

"Oh, it's somewhere about. Where's your pinny Selina?"

Selina looked equally vague. Then she remembered: "The drawer." She pointed to a drawer where the cutlery was kept.

"What a strange place to keep it in." Myra pulled the drawer out.

"Why, there's a pair of nylons here too."

"She tends to stuff things in that drawer, don't worry, they're perfectly clean."

"Well! Nylons in the knife drawer, whatever next?"

And sea boots on the sofa and worms in the bath. Oh auntie, you really should not stay with people like us.

By midday it was almost hot. We planned to do something nice. *Amanda* was seaworthy again and we would take both boats to Pridmouth, a delightful bay lying to the right of the harbour past the two coves, Readymoney and Coombe. It had twin beaches and plenty of sand.

Myra had taken a dislike to *Amanda* (who glared back at her) and she was a bit scared of the water, but I persuaded her to come.

We were all ready to set forth when a dreadful discovery was made. Myra saw it first. She was in the garden bringing in some washing, when she chanced to look beyond the fence that divided our garden from the nine acres of adjoining land.

"I didn't know you had a horse" she said when she came in again.

"We haven't."

"Well there's one just near your garden at the back. It doesn't look very well for it's lying down."

We rushed out at once, followed by Selina at our heels.

When we got to the fence we stopped still, hardly able to believe the sight that confronted us. It was a large pony (or small horse) and it was lying over on its side, some ten feet away from where we stood. It looked lonely and pathetic lying there and the flies were swarming around its head.

"Wait there a minute" said Leo. He climbed over the fence and went towards the animal. After a brief inspection he called out:

"I think it's dead."

"Oh no....how awful." A further inspection confirmed it.

"Yes it's dead. Don't let the kid come over."

"Stay here Selina." I kept a hold on her.

Selina

"How dreadful," said Myra, craning forward to have a good look.

"The poor thing must have stumbled over all that bracken."

"Horsie" said Selina, wondering.

"I think I know where it has come from" said Leo. "That farm at the top. It must have strayed and lost its way and tried to get a drink from the stream. Remember the trouble we had last winter when those cows came down our path?"

"Poor horse" said Selina, now beginning to cry. She loved animals and she didn't really know what was going on. I took her indoors and sat her on my lap for a bit. Presently Leo and Myra came in.

"This has put us in a tight spot" said Leo. "I shall just have to do something....get rid of the thing, as quickly as possible. Sunday too. It couldn't be worse, and bank holiday tomorrow."

"It isn't healthy" said Myra. "This warm weather, especially with a little child about; not at all nice."

"Don't worry, it's going to be dealt with " Leo said, "but the question is how. First I'd better see the farmer. It's really his responsibility. What a bloody awful thing to happen!"

Myra gave him a look.

"I'll go now, meanwhile" he looked at me, "will you try getting on to the medical office of health, we come under the Looe area...he ought to be notified."

I gave Selina a kiss and set her down. "Come to me and I'll read you a nice story" said Myra.

I had no luck in trying to contact the doctor for he was out on a call, so I left a message.

It seemed ages while we waited for Leo to return. He had gone up the spiral path and through the fields.

" I feel awful that this should happen while you're here" I said to Myra. She had finished reading Selina a story and was staring gloomily out of the window.

"First the flies and now this. I wouldn't blame you if you decided to go back."

My aunt gave me a long, fixed look heavy with reproach. "It hurts me" she said "that you should think that I would rush off and leave you when you have trouble."

"Oh no, I didn't mean that, sorry, please don't think...." I apologised all over the place.

169

Autumn Gold

"Unless" she went on, "you want me to go, perhaps I'm in the way?"

"Good heavens no, you mustn't think that." She blew her nose and wiped her glasses. I sensed what was coming.

"I think I shall go to my room for a bit" she said.

"Don't do that. Let's have some coffee....please, cheer ourselves up."

"No thank you. I'm going to lie down for a while. All this worry has brought on one of my bad heads."

I ought to have kept my mouth shut.

****

Nearly an hour later Leo returned, despondent, exasperated.

"No luck" he said. "The farmer can't do anything until after the holiday."

"But that's awful, to have to wait 'till Tuesday."

"Isn't it." He flopped down in a chair and lit a cigarette.

I began to feel frantic. Here we were isolated, with a possible health hazard and literally 'up the creek'.

"The only other thing is to get rid of it myself. The farmer told me that if I didn't want to wait I could dispose of it how I liked."

"But how?"

"I don't know yet....let me think."

"We'll have to do something soon. Oh Leo, I'm so worried. I'm thinking about our health, the baby...."

"Hang on a minute honey." He came over and put his arms around me.

"It's a diabolical thing to have happened, and with your auntie staying here too, but leave it to me - I'll work something out." He went over to the window. Presently he said "I've been thinking....where's auntie by the way?"

"Gone to her room in a huff."

"Oh dear, oh dear." He closed his eyes for a moment and folded his hands in mock prayer. "Never mind, we're not beaten yet, are we baby?"

Selina, playing nearby with a toy pig, looked up and smiled.

"No, I've been thinking" Leo went on "I've got some real pals over at Polruan - remember me telling you about the men who did the improvements and repairs to this place? They're a grand bunch. I've got a feeling they might help out, once they know we're in a tight spot."

In a short while he was off, down the creek in *Amanda*, full steam ahead.

170

Selina

I had heard about the men from Polruan, how they had raised the hut, built partitions and installed a bath and proper sink.. They had made other improvements too. Knowing them to be good natured and reliable, I was not surprised when Leo returned in triumph.

"They're going to do it!" he said. "They'll do the whole job. They'll bring the animal down through our land and lower it down to the cove. I've just seen Silas, he's a marvellous character, he'll organise it. They're coming along soon, about eight of them."

"What a relief. You've done well Leo. And what a good job the tide is just right."

Myra's spirits perked up when she heard the good news. She would keep Selina out of the way while the operation was carried out.

I went down to the cove with Leo to await the arrival of the men. Presently the sound of rich tuneful voices could be heard coming from the water. They were singing old Cornish airs like 'Little eyes I love thee' and 'Twenty Thousand Cornishmen'. Then a large motorboat rounded the bluff. There were several men on board and they were towing something with two objects on it. As the boat came closer to view we saw it was towing a kind of makeshift raft which was carrying an organ and what looked like a large beer barrel. There was a great deal of talk and laughter as the men jumped ashore. Leo was delighted to see them. What was this, a party? The barrel, they told him, was full up with beer. "You wait Mr. Walmsley, some party we'm going to have, I'll tell 'ee boy." We laughed so much that we did not at first see Silas alight from the boat. Then Leo recognised him, wearing a dog collar. "What's all this about a party?" he called out in a booming religious voice. "I'd like to remind you of this solemn occasion that brings us here today."

"This is the funniest thing I've seen yet" said Leo to me "It beats the carnival. Good job your auntie isn't down here!" We all lent a hand at getting the organ and barrel ashore, and then mugs were produced and each one filled and passed round.

Although they arrived in the merriest of moods, and the beer flowed, the men had all their wits about them for their grim task. I didn't want to watch so I went indoors and cut a pile of sandwiches. It was a great relief to have the dead horse removed from our garden, and I was grateful for the help, but I couldn't help feeling sorry for that poor animal lying there in the bright Easter sun.

The job was expertly carried out. Leo gave me an account of it after wards. They had bound the horse with ropes, got it over the fence and pulled it all the way down , carefully avoiding our lawn and the watercress stream by keeping to the left, the Fowey side. It had to pass some rough land and when they reached the bottom they gave a mighty jerk on the rope so that it fell onto the cove. It was then arranged that the animal should be towed up river to Pont where the knackers would collect it.

However Silas had other ideas first. As though from nowhere he produced a surplice and having attired himself he called for quiet and motioned his pals to form a respectful circle around the animal. Then with folded hands and in pious tones he began:

"We bring nothing into this world when we come...." After this someone struck up a hymn on the organ and they sang in their lusty irreverent voices. I don't know what the local vicar would have said.

When the horse had finally been despatched to Pont, the men stopped off on the way back and the revelry began. There was a sing-song around the organ and I brought Selina and the sandwiches down and we joined in. I even persuaded Myra to come down, first dropping a hint to Silas to lose his surplice and dog collar.

It had grown dark by the time the men came to pack up.

"I'll never forget how you helped us" said Leo when we said goodbye to them all. "We were in a tight spot and you came to our rescue."

"Anytime m'andsome."

"And we've all had great fun" I added, "although it was sad about the horse."

"Never mind , m'dear, he be in green pastures now I reckon." He guffawed with laughter at this, then added in a sincere tone:

"There's nothing we wouldn't do for Mr. Walmsley - grand chap he is - and I reckon he'd lend a hand to us if need be. And you know" he added as though divulging a secret," we Cornisnmen have a motto down this part of the world, 'we helps they, they helps we'."

****

CHAPTER XXI.

THE LAST SUMMER

Apart from the drama over the horse, life was fairly peaceful and domestic during this time, although I always had this lurking fear of the future.

Sometimes I was nagged by feelings of guilt. Confined to the kitchen while Leo was working, I might be preparing lunch, and I would glance at Selina sitting on the floor near me, playing with some toy; I would ask myself, have I been selfish to produce a child under these conditions and take her to live up an isolated creek? Life seemed precarious and I would feel overwhelmed at the memory of how I had stood one cold day in a registry office, listened to some words and murmured my responses; then, almost in no time I found myself responsible for this new life. What was in store for our child? She was so vulnerable, so much she had to learn about the beauty and pain of life. At present she was content to trust me. The knowledge of this made me even more anxious for her and I would offer a silent prayer as I scraped away at the carrots.

"Please God protect and look after her, help us to bring her up safely to face the jungle of school, and then the bigger jungle outside, and keep Leo safe when he's out at sea."

Then before growing positively morbid I would be jerked out of it by a tug at my skirt, and looking round, see an anxious face gazing up at me. "Sit on your lap?"

Forget about the carrots!

For a while she would sit, silent, thoughtful, on my lap, sucking her fingers. Had she caught a sense of my gloomy mood I would wonder, over the top of her wispy hair. More guilt feeling now, this time guilty at feeling guilty.

Suddenly she would turn round and face me, her eyes sparkling with fun, and give a quick warm smile like the sun coming out and a look of tolerant perception, a speaking look that said;

"You silly old Goose. What are you quacking and flapping about now? Can't you live in the present like I do? I'm happy. So is Daddy. You cook nice meals for us, we're warm and well fed and we have enough clothes to wear. I think we have a lovely life here. Who cares about the future any way? So belt up Goose, and let's have our dinner."

I would then jump up with a light heart and swing her up in the air, round and round, while she shrieked with delight.

During this time Leo had written **The Happy Ending** and **Sound Of The Sea**, the latter a tale of his boyhood which he dedicated to "Stephanie, Selina and Shawn." Neither of these books were big money spinners and in between novels he wrote articles for *The Yorkshire Post*. He also received a small pension from the war. While we never went short of essentials we could not afford luxuries. Chicken was always a treat. We loved to see a good film at the local cinema but family holidays were out as Leo could not leave the boats. Sometimes I took Selina to stay with my parents, or with Felicity and her family.

In spite of my prayers, the clouds had begun to gather. Winter became more of a problem. One year it was Asian flu, another time measles, and Selina was left with a weak chest and became very wheezy with each infection. Our doctor had to be fetched by Leo in *Amanda*, or else he came across in one of the hire boats. He was quite a sport about it. Once, owing to difficulties with the tide, which was ebbing at the time, Leo couldn't bring his boat full into the cove and there was a small gap between boat and shore. The doctor, immaculate in a dark suit and carrying his black bag, was asked to 'jump for it'.

I began to dread the winters. In 1959 we rented a cottage in Polruan from October to the following March. I enjoyed living in the village, and chatting to the neighbours and shop people. The following year a friend let us stay in her empty house at Readymoney Cove in Fowey.

We knew it had to happen, that we could not carry on indefinitely living up the creek. It was now time to think of packing up. For Leo it was a heart breaking decision. This was the life he loved best, you might say the only one for him. For me it was easy. I could see no alternative and there was none. We had to be practical and face the situation that had got out of hand.

Although Leo took all the major decisions, I was the instigator when it came to this one. The responsibility I felt was to Selina and her future. We couldn't expect our doctor to carry on like a kind of marine goat, leaping from boat to boat to reach us. And if he was a sport about it, we couldn't expect the others in the partnership to be the same - some were wonderful - others kicked.

Then there was the school to think of, looming up ahead like a big question mark. This one I had tried to duck. I was scared. I saw it as a kind of battlefield of viruses. If Selina had already started wheezing through several winters how would she cope when exposed to further infection?

When she approached the critical age of five, I sought advice from experts about keeping her at home for a while and giving her simple lessons. I had already started teaching her. She could already read quite well and write a little, and do very simple sums. They all shook their heads: teachers, doctors, welfare workers, and said the same thing - Selina must go to school.

I could not fight them all, and as Selina herself was keen to go, as children always are at first, it was arranged that she would start, mornings only, at the infant school in Fowey, a month before her fifth birthday. The school was at the top of a big hill, thus adding to the length of a hazardous journey, for she had to go across in *Amanda*. This worked out alright until the weather turned freakish, as it often did, with blustering winds and slanting rain. I think if Leo had harboured any doubts about the wisdom of moving, they must have been dispelled at the sight of his small daughter, clad in oilskins and wellingtons, with her new satchel over her shoulder, crouching hunched up in the tiny cabin while the rain lashed down. And *Amanda* rising and falling, lurching and swaying across the choppy waters of the harbour.

Eventually we had to abandon the idea until the Autumn term, when we hoped to have found somewhere to live on the other side. We had plenty of time to look as this was only April, but we kept a look out for the advertisements in the local paper.

From May onwards the weather changed and became fine. Day after day the sun shone, the creek was still, like glass. The flowers appeared more vivid on the high land, and everything was enhanced and seemed to glow with a deeper beauty because it was threatened. It must have been hard on Leo looking out at this heavenly scene and knowing that time was limited. But he had an ally in Selina who shared his sentiments. "Poor Daddy" she said, "it's not fair."

Well, she was not going to budge! She didn't mind a bit having to cross the harbour to go to school. It was fun. She loved it here and she was going to stay. She would hide herself when the movers came, down by her swing in 'tree-land', her own special retreat. Choo-i would stay with her and they would feed off prawns and mussels.

By now, Leo who had been making enquiries and calling on house agents, had heard of a house to rent at the north end of Fowey. It was only a few yards from Caffa Pill, a little inlet of the river, where boats could safely be moored. This alone made it a hopeful proposition for *Amanda* and the dinghy.

We were keen to see this particular house, which was in Passage Street, a continuation of North Street, and we went along there one afternoon, taking a rather sorrowful Selina with us.

The house was up two flights of stone steps, number twenty-one, and it stood on a terrace among six others all built towards the end of the last century. There was a little patch of garden in front of each house supported by railings going the length of the terrace. The first three houses were divided by an archway leading to the rear parts of the buildings, and by a further flight of steps to their various gardens right at the top.

As soon as we stepped inside I liked the house. It didn't have the charm of a country cottage but there was something solid and safe about it. And there is a certain kind of charm about all houses built in the Edwardian age. The walls were firm and thick and the doors had nice panelling. It was more than big enough for three, with a lounge, a dining room leading into a kitchen and three nice bedrooms - the largest of these overlooked the river giving a fine view and taking in Bodinnick and Ferryside, the house I had first admired, built in front of the rock.

I was in this room, looking out of the window when I sighted one of the big cargo ships. The noise that heralded her arrival, a sort of bleating wail, brought Leo to my side; he had been looking for power points. Selina quickly joined us.

"Isn't this fun?" I said. "We'd see all the big ships from here. How lovely it must be at night when they come in all lit up."

Leo was wishing he had his binoculars to see the name of the ship. "She's on her way to the jetties" he told Selina "to load up with china clay."

Selina was enjoying herself now because it was like playing house. She went from room to room exploring - sometimes coming to grab my hand. "Come and see this one - can this be my room?"

"I like this house" I said to Leo. "We could live here happily."

He was not so enthusiastic for his heart was elsewhere.

"And how easy to keep the boats at Caffa Pill" I went on. "We can still have our trips in *Amanda*." Just then there was a shout from Selina who had gone up another flight of stairs, "Daddy come up here - quick, there's an attic!"

The Last Summer

We followed her up and at the top of the stairs, through a door on the right we saw a lovely spacious room, the ideal place for a writer needing peace and quiet. This I think was one of the deciding factors, for when we got home that evening, we talked it over and agreed to take the house. Another great advantage was the amazingly low rent of two pounds a week.

By June everything was fixed. A contract was drawn up and we would take the house on a ten year lease. The owners agreed to put a dormer window in the attic, which would give an inspiring view, and a rayburn cooker would be installed in the kitchen. We would also have a new bath and loo.

It was fortunate in a way, that the man who owned the pink cottage near to us at Pont Creek, had always wanted to buy our hut. He had a scheme to extend it and build a road down. Now he saw his chance, and took it.

We made the most of what was to be our last summer at the hut. Shawn came for the holidays and we made many trips out to sea. He could now swim the breadth of the creek. Leo had bought him a pair of flippers and a snorkel and he loved being able to tell us what he could see under water. We swam almost greedily in that lovely creek, gathered armfuls of winkles, filled our nets with prawns and stripped the garden bushes of blackcurrants and blackberries. We walked for the last time up the spiral path to Polruan, and pulled in the dinghy up to Pont.

I knew Leo was sad about moving but he kept it to himself. He had this amazing resilience and could always bounce back.

The weather continued fine throughout the summer and we revelled in it. Selina had learnt to swim. She could do the breaststroke and float on her back. She was quite fearless. Even 'Amanda' entered into the spirit of it and took us with a good will to all the favourite places for fishing and picnics. She wasn't so cocky as usual and looked a bit subdued, wondering perhaps about her future.

For me, the future looked as though it could only be brighter. No longer would we be isolated in times of trouble, but live in a little community of warm-hearted people. Selina would make friends at school and cross doctors would sigh with relief at not having to embark across the water.

There would be other advantages too. There was a welled stocked grocers shop just across the raod from the house, and it was only a few minutes walk to the town centre. As for Selina, she would have company on the terrace for there was a family living at the far end who had a little girl just a little older than her.

I pointed out all these advantages to Leo one sunny after-noon two weeks before the move. He was in the workshop making a new fender for Amnda "the other woman".

"And what can stop us from swimming in the creek whenever we like" I went on "we won't be far away from it."

"Yes, we can do that alright. Thank God I'll be able to hang on to the boats. I must have them. It would break my heart to part with dear old Amanda, even though she can be a bitch at times."

"I love the dinghy too. She's a good friend and never lets you down. We ought to give her a name. Let's give her one."

"Selina think of one."

"I say, do you realise how easy it will be to go fishing, as we'll be right near the jetties?"

"What about my swing" said Selina "can we take it with us?"

"Oh, so you've changed your tune have you? You're not supposed to be coming with us. I thought you were going to stay on here with choo-i, both of you living the good life on sea food and wild berries."

Suddenly Leo cried "I've got it!" just as though he had landed a mon-ster bass. His face lit up with joy.

"Yes, I've got it."

"Got what? Don't keep us in suspense."

"So have I" said Selina "I got a name for the . . ."

"Wait a minute . . . I've just thought of an idea for a new book . . . its come to me just like that."

Oh Leo, how lovely. Tell us about it."

"I'm going to write about my second life, about my coming back to live here, and how I set about to re-create this home and make it a paradise for the children. I'm quite excited about it."

"So am I."

"Me too. What is a sec . . ."

"I've even thought of a title. PARADISE CREEK. Do you like that?"

"Perfect. That sounds to me like a really happy title."

"It will be a happy book, my best one yet."

"I got a title too" said Selina "for the dinghy. I want to call her Choo-i." At last we took notice of her.

"Bravo!" said Leo "now that's a splendid idea. I tell you what, we'll go right down now and paint it on. We.ve got some paint in here."

"Talking of titles" I said "I've thought of a name for our new house.

How about 'BRAMBLEWICK'." This was the fictitious name Leo used for Robin Hoods Bay. The idea was well received by them both. They were now rummaging around selecting brushes and paints.

"Selina, pass me that bottle of turps please" said her father "careful now, don't spill . . . thank you, and that rag just behind you."

"Will there be me in your new book?" she asked as she fetched it for him.

"Yes, you and mummie, because it will have a surprise ending."

"And Shawn and Choo-i, are they in it too?"

"Come on" he laughed "I haven't written it yet." he gathered up the paints and gave her a tin to carry.

"We shan't be long" he said to me.

"Come and see when we've finished Mummie."

I watched them as they went happily along the path down to the creek. But perhaps I should call it Paradise Creek, for that is the way I'm always going to remember it.

****

The End